Science
Revision

John Sadler and Emily Clare

Contents

Wanted – do you recognise this cell?

'Today's paper, sir.' Max the housekeeper handed the paper to Izzy's dad, Sir Ralph, who read the headline.

'Good heavens, Izzy, there's been a robbery in our village. Look, there's a photofit of the robber, and a description of him below.'

Have you seen this robber?

He is rectangular in shape, thin skinned with a dark patch in one place and has a long nose-like projection.

He belongs to the group called <u>cells</u>, and his name is root hair cell. Collections of these root hair cells work together and form a <u>tissue</u>. Different tissues have different jobs to do. The root hair cell works underground collecting water and minerals to pass up to the plant.

There are other types of cells known to the police operating in your area — sperm, cilia, ova, muscle and palisade — each has a different job to do.

There is a particularly nasty cell to watch out for, called Salmonella.

Working by himself he poisons people. He belongs to a group called bacteria, and should not be approached.

> **What do you call a group of cells of the same type?**
>
> A tissue...
>
> Bless you!

Identity parade

Link each cell to its correct description by drawing a line. The first one has been done for you.

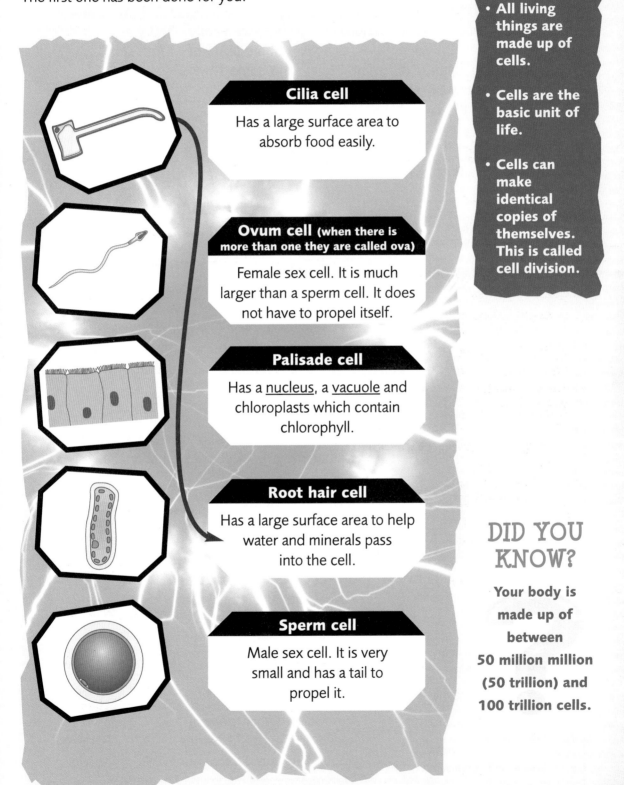

Cilia cell
Has a large surface area to absorb food easily.

Ovum cell (when there is more than one they are called ova)
Female sex cell. It is much larger than a sperm cell. It does not have to propel itself.

Palisade cell
Has a <u>nucleus</u>, a <u>vacuole</u> and chloroplasts which contain chlorophyll.

Root hair cell
Has a large surface area to help water and minerals pass into the cell.

Sperm cell
Male sex cell. It is very small and has a tail to propel it.

• TOP TIPS •

- All living things are made up of cells.

- Cells are the basic unit of life.

- Cells can make identical copies of themselves. This is called cell division.

DID YOU KNOW?

Your body is made up of between 50 million million (50 trillion) and 100 trillion cells.

'Little units of life'

Izzy was sitting by the window, looking out into the garden. Max came and stood beside her and said,
'Amazing isn't it Izzy, all those different plants, birds and that rabbit over there – look – all made from the same things really.'

'What do you mean?' asked Izzy.

'Well, they are all made up of little units of life,' answered Max.

'So', Izzy was thinking out loud, 'are the cells in plants and the cells in animals the same?'

Are we really all made up of the same things?

'I thought you might ask that. How about you look on the Internet and see if you can answer that question yourself?'

This is what Izzy found on her computer by putting in the search string: structure, cell, plant or animal.

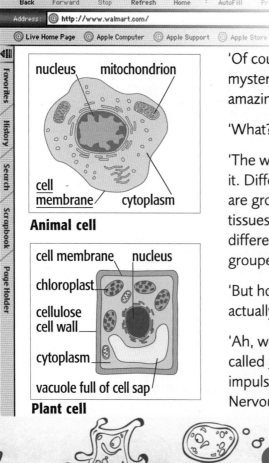

| Back | Forward | Stop | Refresh | Home | AutoFill | Print |

Address: http://www.walmart.com/

Live Home Page   Apple Computer   Apple Support   Apple Store   Microsoft

Animal cell
- nucleus
- mitochondrion
- cell membrane
- cytoplasm

Plant cell
- cell membrane
- nucleus
- chloroplast
- cellulose cell wall
- cytoplasm
- vacuole full of cell sap

'Of course it doesn't stop there,' Max added rather mysteriously. 'Look at that picture on the wall. Isn't it amazing!'

'What?' asked Izzy. 'It's dad when he was younger.'

'The wonderful thing is that you can 'see' it. Different types of cells in your eye are grouped to form different tissues, and all the different tissues are grouped to form an <u>organ</u>.'

'But how does my eye actually see?' asked Izzy.

'Ah, well, another tissue called <u>nervous tissue</u> carries impulses (signals) from your eye to your brain. Nervous tissue is made up of nerve cells.'

Nerve cell
- nucleus
- cytoplasm

Spot the difference

The table lists the features of animal and plant cells.
Some of these features occur only in a plant cell, or only
in an animal cell, or in both animal cells and plant cells.

Put a ✓, or a ✗ in the correct places in the table. The first one has
been done for you.

Feature	Does it occur in plant cells?	Does it occur in animal cells?
cell wall	✓	✗
cell membrane		
cytoplasm		
chloroplast		
nucleus		
vacuole		

• TOP TIPS •

- Plant cells have a cell wall (animal cells do not).

- Cells of the same type group together to make a tissue.

- Several different tissues group together to make an organ, e.g. heart, lungs, eyes, skin.

DID YOU KNOW?

Red blood cells do not have a nucleus.

Hidden message

For each description, write the correct name of the organ in the grid. The first and last letter
of each word has been filled in. The first one has been done for you.

- Pump that keeps the blood moving.
- Site of gas exchange in humans.
- Place where urine is temporarily stored.
- They contract to produce movement in animals.
- Female sex organs, which produce egg cells.

1 H	2 E	3 A	4 R	5 T		
6 L	7	8	9	10 S		
11 B	12	13	14	15	16	17 R
18 M	19	20	21	22	23	24 S
25 O	26	27	28	29	30	31 S

Write the letter from the grid square above that has the same number as the box below.
The answer is an important scientific message. The first word has been done for you.

3 A	6	22

12	29	26	29	8	9

5 T	1 H	29	8	9	31

3 A	28	16

18	13	14	2 E

25	F

21	30	12	6	24

All change!

Izzy and her dad were sitting in the waiting room at the doctor's surgery. Opposite Izzy was a large, colourful poster. It caught her attention, and she studied it carefully.

After seeing the doctor, Izzy went to school. In biology they measured everyone's height and recorded it in a chart.

Height (cm)	Number at height
< 120	2
121–130	3
131–140	5
141–150	8
151–160	6
161–170	3
>171	1

They had to draw a bar graph of their measurements.

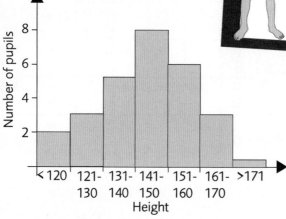

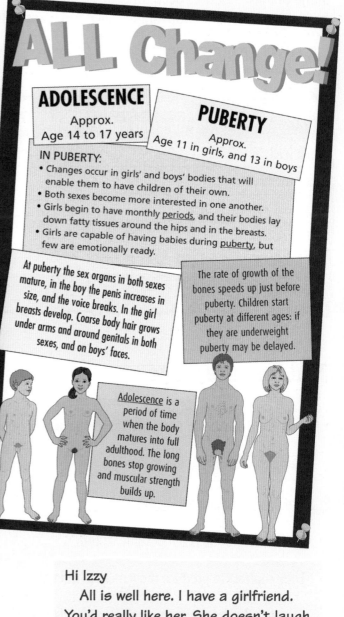

Hi Izzy

All is well here. I have a girlfriend. You'd really like her. She doesn't laugh like the other girls at my voice changing. I've attached a photograph from my 14th birthday party.

When Izzy got home from school, there was an email for her. It was from her cousin Sam.

Izzy looked at the picture. Sam was very different from the last photo she had seen of him. He had a slight moustache and a large Adam's apple. His shoulders looked much broader too.

Mystery family

Solve who A, B, C, D and E are in a family of five using the information below.

Write their names on the graph.

- George is the oldest.
- Mary is the youngest.
- James is the tallest.
- James and Alison are twins.
- Daniel and George are the same height.

TOP TIP

Adolescence is the term used for the period when boys and girls grow from children into adults. The starting of this time is called puberty.

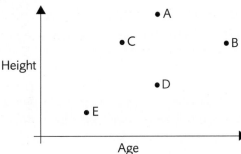

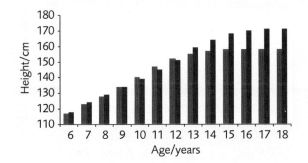

Taller and taller

The bar chart shows the average heights of girls (pink) and boys (blue) between the ages of six and 18 years.

a) (i) At what age is the average height of boys and girls the same?

....

(ii) From the bar chart at what ages are girls taller than boys?

....

(iii) Suggest why girls are taller than boys during this period.

....

b) How much taller (on average) will a 20 year old man be than a 20 year old woman?

....

DID YOU KNOW?

A girl fetus at 20 weeks has between six and seven million eggs. At birth this has reduced to between one and two million. When a girl's periods start the number of eggs has reduced to between 300 000 and 500 000 eggs. Of these only 300 to 400 mature and are released during the woman's fertile lifespan.

Baby talk

Izzy had had a lesson on <u>fertilisation</u> at school. Now at home, her mind wandered off and she imagined fertilisation as an amazing adventure.

She was an <u>ovum</u> in one of the two <u>ovaries</u>. Each month she had noticed other ova around her ripen, and if they didn't meet a sperm, they were lost through the vagina, together with the broken down lining of the <u>uterus</u>, a process called <u>menstruation</u> (or a period). In this month's <u>menstrual</u> <u>cycle</u> she was now ripe and it was her turn. 'Here goes,' she said to herself as she was wafted gently into one of the two long tubes called the <u>oviducts</u>. The oviduct was muscular and lined with cilia and moved her onwards.

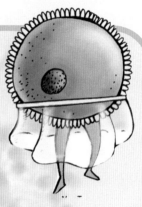

The sperm was tiny. He had a large head and the rest of his body consisted of a tail. He was one of millions of sperm formed inside the <u>testes</u>.

All the sperm were swimming along a tube that led from the testes to the penis and the outside. The penis had become erect and was entering the vagina of the partner. Now in the female they had to pass through a narrowing called the <u>cervix</u>, and then swim on up through the large space in the <u>uterus</u> and then into one of the narrower oviducts – a 30 hour journey!

Many of the sperm perished along the way. One sperm knew he could make it, he was a strong swimmer and he so wanted to be the single sperm that reached the ovum and fused with her.

At last he reached the ovum. He passed through the outer surface to the inside. As he did so his tail fell off. The other hundreds of sperm that had also made it crashed into the ovum but could not follow him inside. He was alone inside the ovum and <u>fertilisation</u> had begun.

He had succeeded. The single cell that he and the ovum had formed was the beginning of a new life. The cell began to divide several times as it continued down the oviduct and into the uterus, where it embedded in the thick, soft lining.

The <u>embryo</u> grew into a <u>fetus</u>. The fetus was fed through the <u>umbilical</u> <u>cord</u>, which was attached to the <u>placenta</u>. The fetus felt very comfortable as it sat snugly in the warmth of a watery liquid. It grew steadily until, after nine months, it had developed into a baby. The baby turned its head downwards in the uterus and two days later was born through the vagina.

Egg timer

Number the drawings 1 to 5 to show the correct order of events in fertilisation.

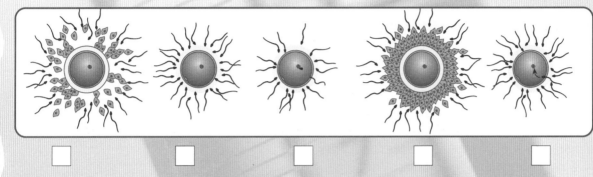

☐   ☐   ☐   ☐   ☐

Born to order

Number the drawings 1 to 4 to show the correct order of events in a growing fetus.

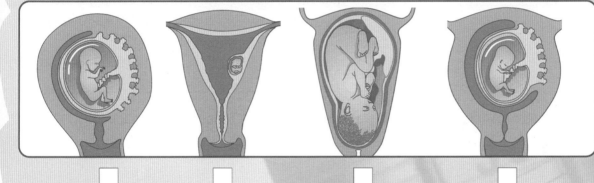

☐   ☐   ☐   ☐

• TOP TIPS •

- Fertilisation occurs when a male sex cell (sperm) joins with a female sex cell (ovum).
- The two main functions of the male reproductive system are to:
  - produce sperm
  - deliver the sperm as close as possible to the ovum.
- The two main functions of the female reproductive system are to:
  - make ova (when there is more than one ovum, they are called ova)
  - provide a safe place for the baby to grow during pregnancy.

DID YOU KNOW?

Some animals, e.g. rabbits, produce several ova at a time. This is why they give birth to a number of babies.

Test your knowledge 1

1 a) The diagram shows an animal cell.

    (i) Match each part of the diagram with its correct name.

    (ii) Match each part to its correct function.

       The first one has been done for you.

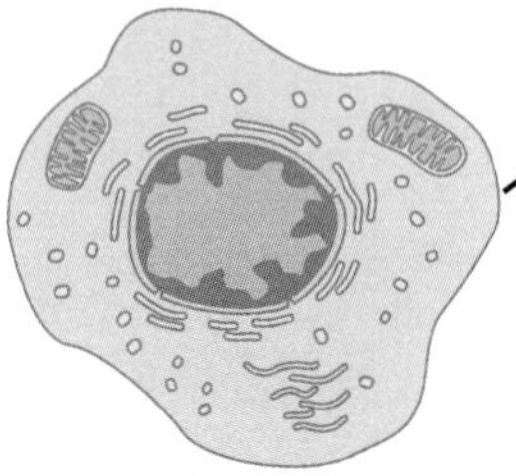

Part name	Function
• cell membrane	• control centre for a cell's activities
• cytoplasm	• holds the cell together and allows nutrients to pass in and waste products to pass out
• nucleus	• makes up all the living material in a cell except the nucleus
• vacuole	• stores water, food and wastes

  b) Name TWO things found in plant cells that are NOT found in animal cells.

    (i) ....

    (ii) ....

(8 marks)

2 The text below describes the menstrual cycle.

Fill in the gaps using only the words and numbers listed below. A word or number may be used once, more than once or not at all.

14 16 28 baby cervix ovary period pregnant puberty urethra uterus vagina

The .... releases an egg (ovum). The lining of the .... gets ready to receive the ovum if it is fertilised. If the ovum is not fertilised the lining breaks up and the woman has a .... The menstrual cycle lasts for about .... days and then it is repeated. It first starts when a girl reaches .... When a woman is .... the menstrual cycles stops. It then re-starts after the .... is born.

(6 marks)

3 The diagram below shows a male and a female.

Label the female F, and the male M.

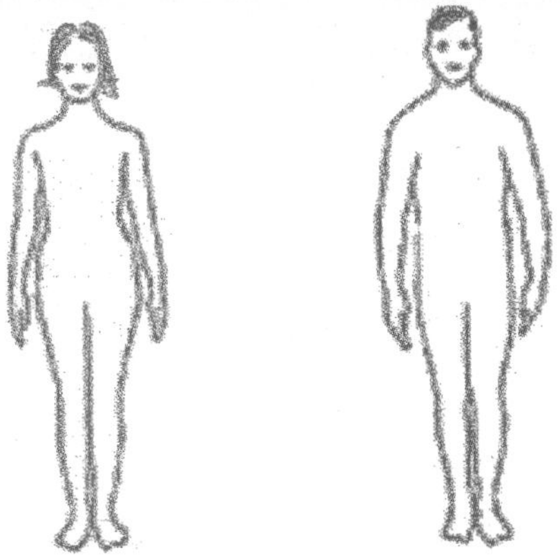

a) Describe how you made your decision.

....

....

b) For boys and girls, give two changes that take place during puberty.

Boys: (i) ....   Girls: (i) ....

(ii) ....   (ii) ....

(6 marks)

4 The diagram below shows four different cells.

The jobs that cells do include:

A   carrying dust and germs away from the lungs
B   helping to contract muscles
C   sending impulses from one part of the body to another
D   swimming towards an egg to help fertilise it

Write the correct letter below each cell to show the job it does.

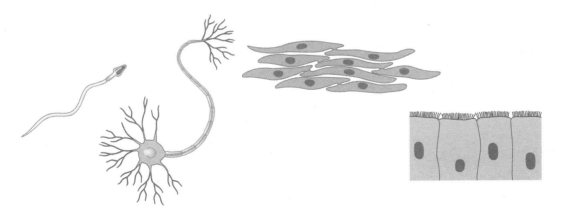

(6 marks)

(Total 26 marks)

Animal magic

Izzy was interested in animals. As well as Spotless, Izzy looked after her two hamsters and her tropical fish. Izzy wrote notes in a large notebook. Here are two of the pages.

MY HAMSTERS

I noticed Meg making a nest last week. I thought she might be getting ready to have babies so I looked on the Internet to see what special care she needed. I found out that I need to feed her eggs and cheese for a few days after the birth to stop her eating her babies!

She's had seven babies in the night!
I have counted 14 teats which the babies feed from. Hamsters suckle their young on milk, like human mothers, except humans have two teats.

MY GUPPIES

The shop assistant at the aquatic centre made sure I bought some male and some female guppies. The males' colours are much brighter than those of the female.

I found some fry (live baby fish) in the water today! I put them in a separate bowl to stop the adults from eating them. Most fish reproduce by <u>external</u> <u>fertilisation</u>. Guppies are different because they breed by <u>internal</u> <u>fertilisation</u>, giving birth to live young, like humans.

Izzy also recorded what she and her dad had seen in their garden pond.

We saw a heron at the pond. I hope it didn't eat too many of the tadpoles! The heron is a <u>predator</u>.

We saw a young adult frog on the bank today. The change from a tadpole to a frog is called <u>metamorphosis</u>. Frogs are <u>amphibians</u>; they live in water and on land.

Find the hidden words

Underline the hidden word in each of these sentences. They can all be found on pages 14 and 15.

1 Are you baking fish Eric?

2 Izzy would be happy if Roger came to see her.

3 The cat's paw needed to be looked at.

4 This ham's terrible, Max. Where did you buy it?

5 Why are you getting up pies from the cellar dad?

Animal differences

Use the information in the table below and the passage on page 15 to answer the questions.

	Dog	Hamster	Guppy	Frog	Human
Life span	9–17 yrs	2 yrs	1.5–3 yrs	10–40 yrs	75–80 yrs
Average litter size	2–10	5–10	4–17	3000	1
Length of pregnancy	58–63 days	18–21 days	1 month	lays eggs	9 months
Nursing period	6–8 weeks	10–21 days	0	0	0.5–2 yrs

Which animals:

1 breed by internal fertilisation? ....
....

2 can survive by themselves as soon as they are born? ....

3 have the longest pregnancy? ....

4 lay many eggs? ....

• TOP TIPS •

- There is a greater chance of survival for fetuses that develop inside the female.

- Animals that fertilise externally produce large numbers of eggs. Animals that fertilise internally produce few eggs.

- When animals such as frogs and butterflies change their form it is called metamorphosis.

DID YOU KNOW?

The first test tube baby was Louise Joy Brown. She was born on 25 July 1978.

Home, sweet home

It was springtime and Izzy was looking out of the window at the garden thinking how lucky she was. There was a wood, a pond, a lawn and some long grass that her dad did not mow. The garden was surrounded by a thick hedge. Each part of the garden had different features that provided different animals and plants with a different <u>habitat</u>.

The swallows had <u>migrated</u> to her garden and were beginning to build nests just below the gutters on the house. How many living things can you spot in the oak tree habitat?

A hedgehog had woken from its <u>hibernation</u> and was resting in the fallen leaves of the oak tree.

The pond was also full of life at this time of year. The picture below shows what Izzy spotted.

What was special about habitats? When she thought about it Izzy realised that they produce food, shelter and a place to bring up babies – rather like her own home.

The animals were adapted to their habitats by having special features. For example, fish have gills so they can breathe under water and fins so they can move in water and a tail to guide them like a rudder on a boat. A bird has wings to fly; squirrels have strong teeth to crack and eat nuts; even earthworms have a tubular muscle structure that contracts and relaxes to move them through the soil.

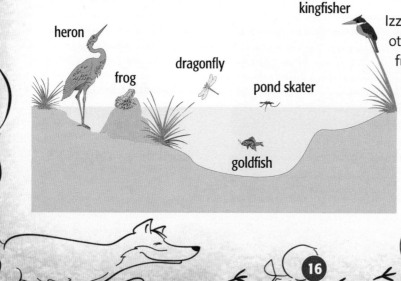

heron
kingfisher
frog
dragonfly
pond skater
goldfish

Izzy thought about habitats in other countries. Polar bears have fur to keep them warm in arctic conditions. Camels in the desert have large humps to store fat. Turtles have special feet so they can swim in the sea and crawl on sand to lay their eggs. Penguins have a thick layer of fat to keep them warm.

Mystery animals

Work out which letters of the alphabet are missing and rearrange them to find TWO animals. Animal 1 is adapted to living in very cold places. Animal 2 is adapted to living on land and in water.

(Hint: work through the alphabet to discover the letters that are missing.)

• TOP TIPS •

- Animals and plants adapt to their environment.
- A habitat is where an animal or plant lives.
- A habitat provides food, shelter and somewhere to reproduce.

C	W	N	B	K	T	J	U	V	Y	C	H
D	Z	I	P	X	Q	I	T	B	M	Z	X
N	Q	J	D	H	M	P	K	Y	T	W	Y

The missing letters are: _ _ _ _ _ _ _ _

Animal 1 is a: _ _ _ _

Animal 2 is a: _ _ _ _

DID YOU KNOW?

There are about:

- **9700 different types of birds**
- **28 000 different types of fish**
- **44 000 different types of spiders**
- **1 000 000 different types of insects.**

Fill in the gaps

Fill in the missing words to reveal the facts.

1 A _ _ _ _ _ _ _ _ is a precise place, e.g. ponds and seashores, where plants and creatures live.

2 These sentences are about adapting to environmental conditions.

a) In winter some birds _ _ _ _ _ _ _ to warmer places.

b) Camels can survive in deserts for a long time without _ _ _ _ _ .

c) Dormice and hedgehogs spend the cold winters _ _ _ _ _ _ _ _ _ _ _ .

d) A fish has _ _ _ _ to help it swim in water.

e) In order to survive the cold winter, cats and dogs grow more _ _ _ _ .

Who ate Peter Pigeon?

Each day, Izzy's dad liked to listen to the 'coo-coo' of the wood pigeon sitting in the oak tree at the bottom of his garden. He had nicknamed the pigeon Peter.

Out for a stroll around the garden before lunch, Izzy's dad noticed Spotless getting excited with his nose to the ground under the oak tree. There in the grass were some scattered grey feathers and the remains of Peter Pigeon. Spotless was now very excited and he shot off on a scent trail and ran right through a well-worn tunnel in the hedge.

Izzy's dad called sharply 'Spotless, come here now!'

He was by the gap in the hedge waiting for Spotless to return, when he noticed a strand or two of reddish-brown, coarse hair snagged on a twig at the entrance to the tunnel. He carefully collected the hair, then he went back and picked up Peter's remains. At last Spotless returned and the pair went inside.

Later that day, Izzy and her dad took the remains to a friend who lived nearby and worked as a forensic scientist. After carrying out various tests it was found that Peter had eaten earthworms for supper. The forensic scientist mapped out what he thought had happened. He called it a <u>food</u> <u>chain</u>. He explained that after the pigeon had eaten earthworms for his supper a fox had found Peter during the night and had eaten most of him. He said that this was a 'food chain'.

'What do earthworms eat?' asked Izzy.

'Grass or leaves,' answered the scientist, who added 'and before you ask me, no, grass doesn't exactly eat; it makes its food by using energy from the sunlight falling on its leaves to turn water and carbon dioxide into sugars in a process called <u>photosynthesis</u>. Grass is called the <u>producer</u> in the food chain. Earthworms, pigeons and foxes are called <u>consumers</u>.'

What's for dinner, Max?

Food chain, Sir

Who's eating who?

A forensic scientist drew pictures of everything in a food chain. By drawing arrows, show the correct order of the food chain.

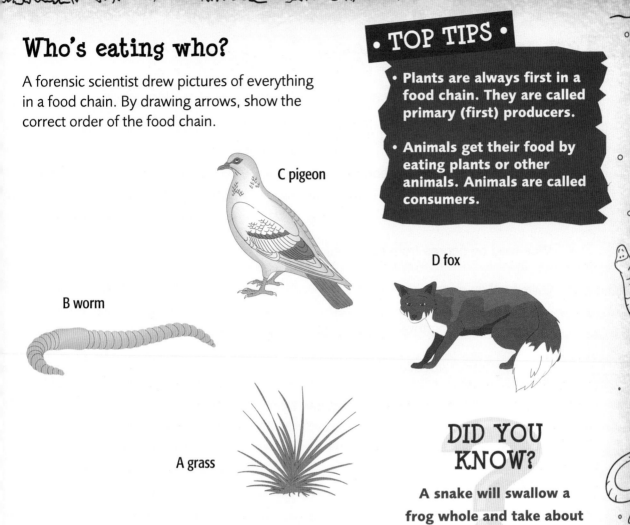

C pigeon

D fox

B worm

A grass

DID YOU KNOW?

A snake will swallow a frog whole and take about 50 hours to digest it.

Unscrambling

Rearrange the letter groups below in the correct order to find the names of an insect, two birds and a plant that make up a food chain.

AACEILLPRRT _ _ _ _ _ _ _ _ _ _ _   AOPRRSW _ _ _ _ _ _ _

AKHW   _ _ _ _   EERT   _ _ _ _

Now write the four names in the correct boxes below to make a food chain.

	→	→	→

Producers make their own food. Write the name of the producer in the above food chain.

Producer: ....

Test your knowledge 2

1   A scientist made the following notes on his observations about food chains.

- Earthworms and slugs feed on dead leaves and grass.

- Foxes feed on mice, hedgehogs and pigeons.

- Hedgehogs feed on slugs.

- Mice feed on acorns from oak trees.

- Owls feed on mice.

- Pigeons feed on earthworms, spiders and slugs.

- Spiders feed on woodlice.

- Woodlice feed on dead leaves from oak trees.

a) Fill in the gaps in these food chains.

(i)   acorns → .... → owl

(ii) grass → .... → pigeon → owl

(iii) .... → slugs → hedgehog → ....

(iv) .... → woodlice → .... → .... → fox

b) Name the producer in food chain (i).

    ....

c) (i) Name TWO animals that eat slugs.

         .... and ....

    (ii) Name ONE animal that eats pigeons.

         ....

d) Which animal might disappear from the garden if the oak tree did NOT produce
    any acorns?

    ....

(13 marks)

2 The photograph shows a frog swimming. A frog can live on land as well as in water.

a) What type of animal is a frog?

....

b) From the photograph give two features that allow the frog to move quickly and easily through water.

Feature 1: ....

Feature 2: ....

c) Give TWO reasons why the ability of a frog to swim quickly helps it to survive.

Reason 1: ....

Reason 2: ....

d) A frog can lay up to 4000 eggs at one time. The jelly around the eggs helps to keep them warm. It also helps prevent fish from eating them.

(i) How are the eggs fertilised?

....

(ii) What is the advantage of laying so many eggs?

....

(iii) Suggest why the jelly might prevent fish from eating the eggs.

....

....

....

e) In a river-bank habitat frogs eat slugs and slugs eat plants. Complete the table below to show what changes would occur to the number of plants, slugs and frogs if the changes in column 1 were made.

Change made:	Number of plants	Number of frogs	Number of slugs
increase number of frogs	increases		
increase number of slugs		increases	
increase number of plants			

(13 marks)

(Total 26 marks)

Variety is the spice of life

Izzy was watching Spotless in the garden. When Dylan, the ginger cat, came into the garden Spotless didn't notice it at first so Izzy had time to compare them.

Spotless was similar to Dylan in many ways, e.g. they both had eyes, ears, a tail and hair. But in other ways they were very different, e.g. Dylan meowed and spat and Spotless barked and growled; Dylan purred and Spotless didn't. Dylan knew how to clean himself; Spotless was always put in a bath and given a good scrub. Spotless was larger than Dylan.

I do look a bit like you...

At that moment Spotless spied the cat and chased him out of the garden!

Izzy decided to compare herself with the dog. She thought we both have hair (but I have a lot less than Spotless), and we both breathe through our lungs. Our mothers gave birth to us (although Spotless was one of six and I was the only one). When we were young we fed on milk provided by our mothers. We are both <u>mammals</u>. The main difference is that I walk on two legs and Spotless walks on four. That is called <u>variation</u>.

Izzy went into the kitchen where her dad and Max were having a cup of tea. She compared herself to her father. They both had straight hair and their noses were the same shape. Her hair was much fairer – in fact it looked like her mother's hair. Izzy had <u>inherited</u> some features from her dad and some from her mum.

No spots at all...

Face up to it

Each quadruplet has inherited only one facial feature from each of their grandparents. In the diagram below fill in the missing face to show what the baby might look like.

Do you square up?

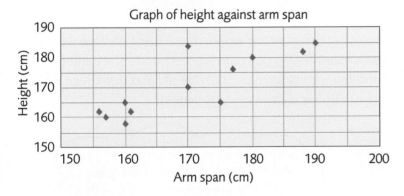

Graph of height against arm span

Arm span is the distance from fingertip to fingertip when the arms are outstretched.

Draw a line showing height = arm span.

a) Suggest the height of someone with an arm span of 165 cm.

  ....

b) How many points are:

   (i) above the line? ....
   (ii) below the line? ....

c) Circle the point that may have been measured incorrectly.

d) What can you say about the relationship of a person's arm span and their height? ....

DID YOU KNOW?

The sex of a pearl oyster can change; its sex depends on its age, and the surrounding water conditions.

In a class of their own

Izzy decided to classify everything in the pond by what it eats. This is what she drew.

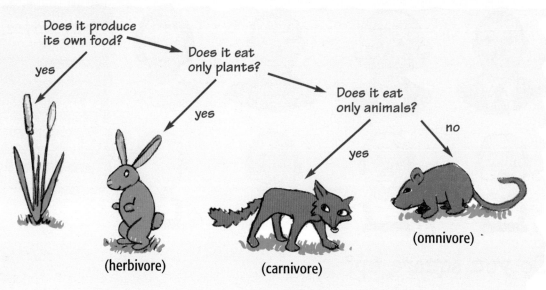

Izzy wondered how to classify all the living things in the world. The easiest division would be animals and plants. These are two examples of <u>Kingdoms</u>. In her bedroom, she looked up 'classification' in her biology book and found that animals could be divided into those with backbones (<u>vertebrates</u>) and those without backbones (<u>invertebrates</u>).

Vertebrates can be sub-divided into fish, amphibians, reptiles, birds and mammals.

Classifying invertebrates is more complicated. Examples of the divisions are worms; insects; spiders; molluscs; e.g. scallops and <u>crustaceans</u>, e.g. crabs.

Plants can be divided into those that make seeds, e.g. grasses and those that do not, e.g. ferns.

> I like the idea of belonging to the meat eaters, or carnivores group. And I like sharing the group with a lion. But I'm not so sure I like having a cat in the same group...

Classifieds

Add ONE letter to each of the sets of letters below to answer each clue.

List the new letters and discover the clue to classifying living things.

BACBONE	another name for the spine
CONFERS	group consisting of large trees with needle-shaped leaves, e.g. pine
FUGI	yeast and mushrooms belong to this group
ALAE	simple plants that live in fresh water or seawater, e.g. seaweeds
SEES	they develop from fertilised ovules in plants
MLLUSCS	snails, limpets and mussels belong to this group
OSSES	simple plants, with no proper roots, that grow in damp places
FIH	a vertebrate that lives in water

The word is: ☐ ☐ ☐ ☐ ☐ ☐ ☐ ☐

What are we?

Using the description given in the middle column and the classification key on the opposite page, identify each of the living things in the table as either plant, <u>carnivore</u>, <u>herbivore</u> or <u>omnivore</u>.

Name	Description	Plant, carnivore, herbivore or omnivore?
dragonfly nymph	attacks other animals and small fish	
duckweed	its leaves float on surface	
goldfish	eats anything from duckweed to smaller fish	
mayfly nymph	feeds on plants	
pondweed	grows below the surface	
water boatman	feeds on decaying matter	
watermite	sucks the blood of larger animals	

• TOP TIPS •

- **Living things can be divided into animals and plants.**
- **The animal kingdom can be divided into vertebrates and invertebrates.**
- **Vertebrates can be sub-divided into fish, mammals, reptiles, amphibians and birds; invertebrates can be sub-divided into groups including molluscs, spiders, insects and crustaceans.**
- **Plants can be divided into those that produce seeds and those that do not.**

Test your knowledge 3

1 A girl from Mozambique was writing a letter to send to her new penfriend. This is how she described herself.

My name is Cecilia Baptisto	I am 15 years old	I have a turned up nose
I am 1.65 m tall	I have brown eyes	I have a scar on my knee
I am black	I have long black hair	I speak Portuguese

a) Select THREE features that Cecilia inherited from her parents that will NOT have been affected by her environment.

(i) ....

(ii) ....

(iii) ....

b) Select THREE features that might have been affected by both inherited and environmental factors.

(i) ....

(ii) ....

(iii) ....

Cecilia included a bar chart showing the heights of the girls in her class.

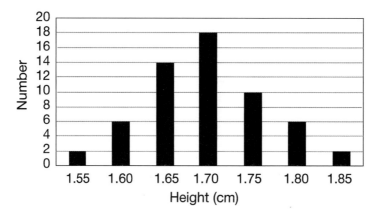

c) (i) How many girls were taller than Cecilia? ....

(ii) Name TWO other features of the girls in Cecilia's class that would show a similarly shaped bar chart.

Feature 1: ....

Feature 2: ....

(9 marks)

2   a)   Use the key below to identify these six invertebrates. Write the correct letter A, B, C, D, E or F in the boxes at the end of the key.

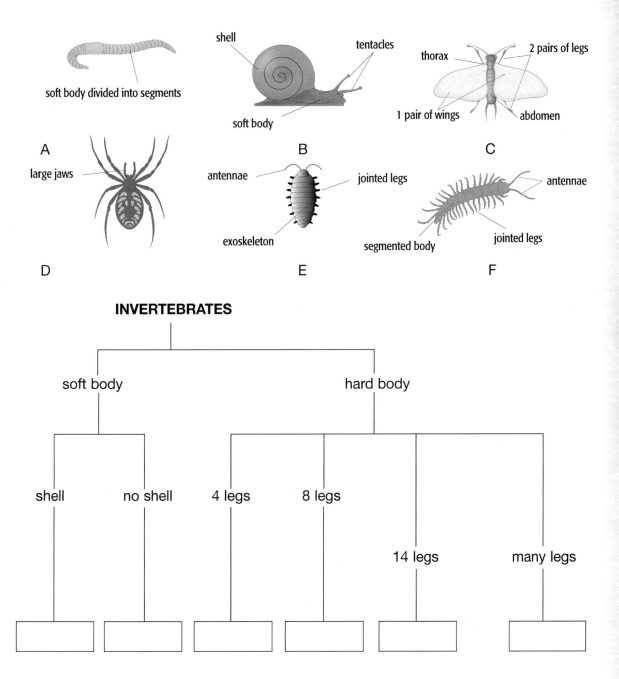

b)   Name the invertebrates A B, C, D, E and F.
     Two have been done for you.

A		B		C	Mayfly
D		E		F	Centipede

(10 marks)

(Total 19 marks)

Bitter sweet

Izzy's dad took his first sip of wine and spluttered, 'Ugh, this wine tastes bitter and sharp – a bit like vinegar in fact.'

'I think the bottle may have been open for a while,' suggested Max.

'Like the milk that tasted sour because we left it out of the fridge for too long,' added Izzy.

'Yes,' answered her dad. 'When I was at school I studied Latin. It is a very interesting language because many of the words we use today stem from it. The Latin word *acidus*, for example, means sour. The English language uses the word <u>acid</u> for a sour-tasting substance. Sour milk contains lactic acid and my wine has turned to acetic acid, which is another name for ethanoic acid.'

'Lemons, oranges, limes, tangerines and grapefruit taste sour and bitter – do they contain acids?' asked Izzy.

'Yes, they contain citric acid. That's why they're called citrus fruits. Many fruits and vegetables contain another acid too, called ascorbic acid or vitamin C.'

'If you leave tea to stand for a long time it tastes bitter because it forms tannic acid,' Max added.

'I know another one,' said Izzy. 'We learnt about it at school. It is found in the stomach and helps to break food down during digestion; it's called hydrochloric acid.'

'The interesting thing about acids,' Ralph added 'is that they are <u>neutralised</u>, or cancelled out, by substances called <u>alkalis</u>. Alkalis are <u>bases</u>, for example, metal oxides, that are <u>soluble</u> in water.'

'Mmm', said Max 'I can think of some household cleaning substances that contain alkalis. Alkalis make substances feel soapy – detergents and bath cleaning creams are examples. Ammonia solution and Milk of Magnesia are two examples of alkalis used in medicines.'

'And because alkalis neutralise acids, if you get a bee sting, which is acid, put ammonia solution on your skin and if you are stung by a wasp which is alkali, put on vinegar. I remember it by 'A for B' – ammonia for bees and 'V for W' – vinegar for wasps,' said Ralph.

Wordsearch

Find THREE common acids and TWO common alkalis hidden in the grid. Words may read down, across or diagonally.

A	P	X	Z	D	L	M	D
M	S	A	C	E	T	I	C
M	H	C	I	T	R	I	C
O	T	F	O	E	O	V	K
N	R	N	M	R	L	X	W
I	P	T	S	G	B	Y	K
A	G	X	F	E	C	I	T
H	W	S	G	N	W	A	C
K	H	X	H	T	Z	X	D

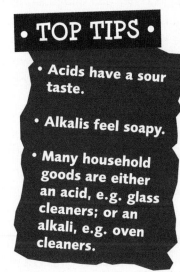

• TOP TIPS •

• Acids have a sour taste.

• Alkalis feel soapy.

• Many household goods are either an acid, e.g. glass cleaners; or an alkali, e.g. oven cleaners.

Sorting substances

Write A for acid, B for alkali or C for neutral by each of these common substances.

apple		fruit juice		sugar solution	
common salt		oven cleaner		toothpaste	
detergent		pineapple		vinegar	
drain cleaner		soda water		water	

DID YOU KNOW?

• Farmers spread alkaline calcium oxide (commonly known as lime) on their fields to neutralise acidic soil.

• When lime is heated strongly it gives off a very bright light. The stages in theatres used to be lit by light given off by heated lime. People on the stage were said to be 'in the limelight'.

• In the past, sailors on long voyages had to make sure that they had a good supply of oranges and other citrus fruits on their ships. The fruits are a good source of ascorbic acid (vitamin C) which is used by the body to keep skin tissues healthy. Without vitamin C, sailors suffered from bleeding gums and other symptoms of a disease called scurvy.

Indicators

Izzy and her dad had just finished eating dinner. One of the vegetables was red cabbage – not Izzy's favourite and she left some of it. She scraped it off her plate and put the plate in the sink. She added detergent and water and, to her surprise, the mixture turned green. She knew that detergents were alkaline and that vinegar was acidic, so she added some vinegar from the larder to the red cabbage juice in the sink and it turned red.

Max told her that other substances change colour, for example beetroot, black tea, blackberries, turmeric, cherries and even onion skins, and that these substances are natural indicators. He also said that there is an indicator made from lichen (a plant that grows on the bark of trees, concrete and stone) called litmus. It turns red in acid solutions and blue in alkalis.

Later in the year, Izzy learnt about other indicators at school, e.g. methyl orange (turns red in acid and yellow in alkali), phenolphthalein (turns colourless in acids and pink in alkalis) and Universal Indicator. This is a mixture of indicators that changes colour according to the pH of a solution. There is a scale 1 to 14, called the pH scale. If a solution is strongly acidic it has a low pH, and if it is strongly alkaline the pH is high.

pH	0, 1, 2	3, 4	5, 6	7	8, 9, 10	11, 12	13,14
colour							

←—— increasing acidity   neutral   increasing alkalinity ——→

At the end of the lesson one teacher gave out pH papers to test the acidity and alkalinity of substances found in the home. The class was warned not to test substances that had the following warning symbols on their containers. This is because very strong acids and alkalis can be harmful to health.

Substance is harmful/irritant

Substance is corrosive

The picture on the label of one of the household cleaners that Izzy tested was of a rainbow and the Sun. Amazingly, the colours of the rainbow are the same as those used to indicate pH!

Rainbow riddle

Add VOWELS to the following letters to make the colours of the rainbow (and of pH paper).

colour:

RD ....

RNG ....

YLLW ....

GRN ....

BL ....

NDG ....

VLT ....

What is it?

pH	Substance tested
14	oven cleaner
13	soap flakes
12	
11	detergent
	drain cleaner
10	washing soda
	Milk of Magnesia
9	soap
8	toothpaste
	blood
7	water
	common salt
6	milk
5	tea
4	vinegar
	orange juice
3	coca cola
2	lemon juice
1	

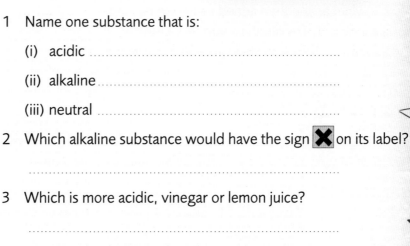

• **TOP TIPS** •

- **Pure water is neutral. It has a pH of 7.**

- **Acids have a pH less than 7. The lower the number the stronger the acid.**

- **Alkalis have a pH greater than 7. The higher the number the stronger the alkali.**

1   Name one substance that is:

(i)   acidic ....

(ii) alkaline...

(iii) neutral ....

2   Which alkaline substance would have the sign ✖ on its label?

....

3   Which is more acidic, vinegar or lemon juice?

....

4   What would be the colour of methyl orange in:

(i)   white vinegar? ....

(ii) Milk of Magnesia? ....

DID YOU KNOW?

Some plants will only thrive (grow well) in acid soil, e.g. heather. The flowers of the hydrangea plant are natural indicators. When grown in alkaline soil the flowers are pink, and when grown in soil free from lime the flowers are blue.

A neutral solution

Izzy had a tummy ache and heartburn ('hot' feeling in the throat and chest area). There was too much acid in her stomach which can be caused by eating too many acidic, or spicy foods. Max fetched the Milk of Magnesia (an <u>antacid</u>) and advised her to take some. Izzy read the label carefully: *'Milk of Magnesia Liquid (Magnesium Hydroxide) – Gentle, soothing relief for upset stomach and indigestion.'* She swallowed a teaspoonful of the chalky-tasting liquid as directed.

Izzy thought she knew why the Milk of Magnesia helped her sore stomach. In order to test her hypothesis (idea) she carried out a simple experiment. She filled a drinking glass half-full with white vinegar and then added some red cabbage-juice indicator. The liquid turned red. Using a teaspoon she slowly added some Milk of Magnesia and stirred the mixture. After adding about five teaspoonfuls the indicator turned green. Izzy now added more teaspoonfuls of white vinegar. After 11 teaspoonfuls had been added the liquid turned to red again.

The Milk of Magnesia had neutralised the vinegar. Izzy's hypothesis has been correct – the Milk of Magnesia acted by neutralising the acid in her stomach.

At school Izzy had used a pH meter connected to a computer so that a graph of pH could be drawn as an acid was added to an alkali. Here is the page from her school book.

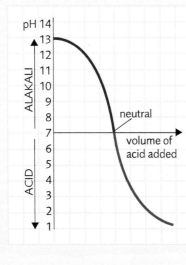

Neutralisation experiment

The pH at the start was 13 (very alkaline). When the acid was added the pH started to fall. We were told that at pH 7 the solution was neutral. When more acid was added the pH dropped to 1 (a strong acid). We also put pH indicator in the solution so that we could watch the colour changes. At pH 13 it was purple, at pH 7 green and at pH 1, red. The reaction is called <u>neutralisation</u>.

Danger signs

All chemicals are labelled. This helps emergency workers decide how to act at an accident site where chemicals are involved.

• TOP TIPS •

- The reaction between an acid and an alkali is called **neutralisation**.

- An **antacid** is any substance that neutralises stomach acid.

Colour	Meaning	0	1	2	3	4	
red	fire hazard; flash point	will not burn	above 93 °C	below 93 °C	below 38 °C	below 23 °C	
blue	health hazard	no hazard	slightly hazardous	hazardous	extremely hazardous	deadly	
yellow	reactivity	stable	unstable if heated	violent chemical	shock or heat may explode	may explode	
white	specific hazard	OXY oxidiser	ACID	ALK alkali	ALK alkali	COR corrosive	₩ use no water

Using the key above, describe what the hazard symbol on the left tells firemen about a chemical stored in a building.

....

....

....

DID YOU KNOW?

The word 'alkali' comes from the Arabic word *Al-kali* meaning wood ashes. Alkalis were once obtained from wood ashes.

Be a detective!

A keen gardener kept a large sack of calcium oxide (lime) in his garden shed which he put on the soil in his vegetable patch in the spring. (His vegetables didn't grow well in an acid soil and the lime neutralised it.) One day the gardener found his shed door wide open, and his sack of calcium oxide missing. He telephoned the police and told them who he suspected. On paying a visit to the suspect's house the police found a white powder in his shoes. Mr C Rook, the suspect, said that he had put talcum powder in his shoes because they were too tight.

What test could you do to see if Mr C Rook was telling the truth?

....

....

....

Test your knowledge 4

1 Milk of Magnesia is used to relieve indigestion. Its two main ingredients are magnesium hydroxide and purified water. Magnesium hydroxide has the following properties:

- it is tasteless

- it is odourless (has no smell)

- it is not very soluble in water and forms a solution with a pH of 9

- it is not poisonous

- it is a white solid.

Use the list above to answer the following questions.

a) (i) Is Milk of Magnesia acidic, alkaline or neutral?

....

(ii) From the list choose TWO properties of Milk of Magnesia that show that it can safely be used to relieve indigestion.

Property 1: ....

Property 2: ....

b) A substance **X** can also be used in indigestion tablets. Give TWO properties of **X** that show that it can be used to relieve indigestion.

(i) ....

(ii) ....

c) Milk of Magnesia is a suspension (an insoluble substance in a liquid, e.g. muddy water). What is the difference between a suspension and a solution?

....

....

....

(7 marks)

2 Use the information in the table to answer the questions below.

Indicator	Colour of indicator in solution of pH													
	1	2	3	4	5	6	7	8	9	10	11	12	13	14
bromothymol blue	yellow			green		blue								
litmus	red					purple		blue						
methyl orange	red			orange		yellow								
phenolphthalein	colourless							pale pink			red			

a) What is the colour of each indicator in a neutral solution?

bromothymol blue: ....   litmus: ....

methyl orange: ....   phenolphthalein: ....

b) Complete the following table to:

(i) show the colour of each indicator in each substance
(ii) state whether each substance is acidic, neutral or alkaline.

Substance	Colour of indicator				Acidic, neutral or alkaline?
	bromothymol blue	litmus	methyl orange	phenolphthalein	
white vinegar	green		orange		
oven cleaner		blue			
orange juice	yellow				acidic
milk		purple			
ammonia solution				red	

c) Circle the most likely pH of a solution made by mixing together equal amounts of white vinegar and ammonia solution.

3   5   7   9   11

d) Hydrochloric acid has a pH of 1.
What would be the colour of a mixture of methyl orange and litmus in hydrochloric acid?

....

e) How would you measure the pH of a coloured substance such as red ink?

....

(24 marks)

(Total 31 marks)

What's done cannot be undone

It was the school holidays and Izzy had taken Spotless for a walk in the wood near to her house. It had rained during the night and in the mud Izzy found some paw prints left by animals. She decided to make plaster casts of the prints.

She went to the shed and found some Plaster of Paris (a fine powder), a bucket and a watering can, which she filled with water. Back in the woods she mixed some Plaster of Paris with some water in the bucket and stirred the mixture with a stick. The mixture got hot and its <u>volume</u> increased. She poured the mixture into each print and then waited for it to set before carrying the casts to the house. Izzy made drawings of the prints and wrote a description of each.

In the afternoon, Izzy was baking a cake in the kitchen with Max. She put the ingredients on the table – water, milk, flour, eggs, butter, sugar and baking powder. As she opened the baking powder some of it spilt into the water. Immediately it started to fizz.

Max explained that there was a <u>chemical</u> <u>reaction</u> (change) taking place in the bowl between the water and the baking powder.

'Carbon dioxide gas is given off. This happens in the cake mixture when it is being baked. It makes the cake rise leaving it nice and light to eat.'

Max added, 'When you made the plaster casts this morning the mixture got hot. That was also a chemical reaction. Chemical reactions cannot be reversed. When you've made your cake, you can't get back the original ingredients. Just as you can't get back the Plaster of Paris powder.'

Max showed Izzy a trick. He mixed together some salt and pepper and asked Izzy to separate them.

'It will take for ever,' said Izzy.

'Oh no it won't,' said Max. 'Comb your hair with your plastic comb. Now hold it over the mixture.'

Izzy was amazed; the pepper was attracted to the comb and the salt stayed on the table.

'There you are,' said Max. 'That's an example of a <u>physical</u> <u>change</u>. After mixing, it is possible to get back the original substances.'

'Rusting must be a chemical change,' said Izzy.

'Yes,' said Max. 'I wish I could reverse the rusting on my old car.'

Paws for thought

Link each paw print to its correct description by drawing a line. The first one has been done for you.

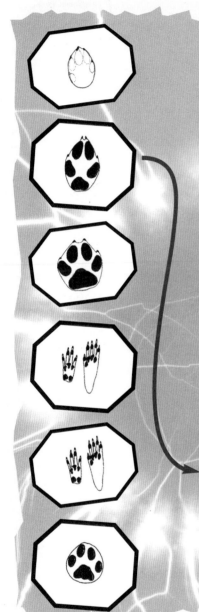

Hedgehog
The front foot is wider that the back foot. The thumb is faint.

Cat
Almost circular showing four toes. No claw marks (they are pulled in when a cat walks).

Squirrel
Moves by hopping, so prints appear in groups. There is no thumb on front foot.

Dog
Like a fox, but pads are bigger. Claw marks can usually be seen.

Fox
Like a dog, but narrower. Longer claw marks than a dog.

Rabbit
Pointed foot. Pads are not very clear. Claw marks can usually be seen.

DID YOU KNOW?

Plaster of Paris is a mineral called gypsum. The fine white powder was first found in large quantities near the French city of Paris, hence its name.

Physical or chemical?

For each action, write P to indicate a physical change, or C to indicate a chemical change.

a) baking a cake   . . . .
b) boiling an egg   . . . .
c) burning a match   . . . .
d) dissolving sugar in water   . . . .
e) melting candle wax   . . . .

Show your metal

Izzy learnt why Max's car made from iron had <u>rusted</u> and her dad's car made from aluminium had not. It was to do with the type of <u>metal</u> used to make the cars. Different metals have different <u>reactivities</u>.

Max explained that there were tests that could be done to see which metals reacted and which did not, e.g. adding an acid to a metal.

Izzy's dad said that he could recall that when he added hydrochloric acid to magnesium, they reacted. The piece of metal disappeared and the solution got warm. Bubbles of gas formed and when a glowing splint was held over the gas it burnt with a...

'Pop!' interrupted Izzy, 'That means it's hydrogen.'

Max then wrote a chemical equation to show what happens in the reaction.

> magnesium + hydrochloric acid → hydrogen + magnesium chloride

Izzy's dad added that other metals did not react with acid, e.g. copper and silver. They had also reacted acids with metal carbonates. He had used limestone (calcium carbonate). This time the gas given off turned limewater cloudy white.

'It was carbon dioxide,' Izzy felt pleased with herself for knowing this too.

'And this,' added Max 'is the chemical equation for the reaction.'

> calcium carbonate + hydrochloric acid → carbon dioxide + water + calcium chloride

Izzy fetched the pot of baking powder and read the ingredients, which included bicarbonate of soda (sodium hydrogencarbonate) and tartaric acid. An acid with hydrogencarbonate gives off carbon dioxide.

> sodium hydrogencarbonate + tartaric acid → carbon dioxide + water + sodium tartrate

Izzy also remembered her teacher burning metals in air. Magnesium burnt very brightly, just like a firework. Metals react with oxygen in the air to form oxides. Metal oxides are bases, which make alkalis when dissolved in water.

> magnesium + oxygen → magnesium oxide

When iron rusts, it reacts with oxygen and water vapour in the atmosphere.

Metal detector

Solve the clues and fill in the missing letters to find the names of the metals.

The first one has been done for you.

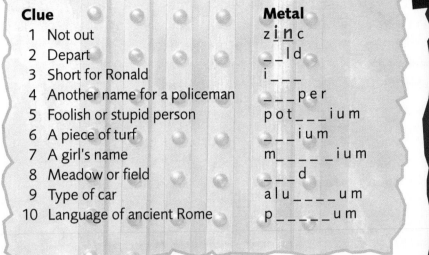

Clue	Metal
1 Not out	z i n c
2 Depart	_ _ l d
3 Short for Ronald	i _ _ _
4 Another name for a policeman	_ _ _ p e r
5 Foolish or stupid person	p o t _ _ _ i u m
6 A piece of turf	_ _ _ i u m
7 A girl's name	m _ _ _ _ _ i u m
8 Meadow or field	_ _ _ d
9 Type of car	a l u _ _ _ _ u m
10 Language of ancient Rome	p _ _ _ _ _ u m

• TOP TIPS •

- When a metal reacts with hydrochloric acid one of the products is hydrogen.

- When a carbonate reacts with hydrochloric acid one of the products is carbon dioxide.

- Hydrogen burns with a 'pop'.

- Carbon dioxide turns limewater cloudy white.

Test your metal

These metals are very reactive:

calcium   magnesium   potassium   sodium   iron

This metal forms a protective oxide layer and therefore appears to be unreactive:

aluminium

These metals are unreactive:

copper   gold   silver   platinum

DID YOU KNOW?

Salt speeds up the rusting process. This is why cars rust faster when they are kept near the coast.

a) Name a metal that rusts. ....

b) Name the silver-white metal used for making pots and pans. ....

c) What metal is used in electric wires? ....

d) Name a metal used for making jewellery. ....

e) Complete these word equations:

   (i) calcium + hydrochloric acid → calcium chloride + ...

   (ii) sodium + ... → sodium oxide

Burning the candle at both ends

Coal fires heated Izzy's house. Some of her friends' houses in the village had gas central heating and others had oil central heating. Izzy's dad said that their house was very old so it would be too expensive to have central heating put in. Coal and gas are <u>fuels</u>. Fuels provide <u>energy</u>. Coal and gas are <u>non-renewable</u> sources of energy. They formed in the Earth millions of years ago and they are made mainly of carbon. Izzy was beginning to like the idea of word equations. She had a go at writing the chemical equation for coal burning in air.

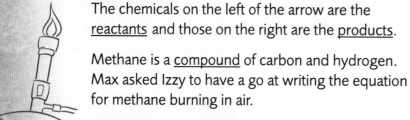

carbon + oxygen → carbon dioxide

The chemicals on the left of the arrow are the <u>reactants</u> and those on the right are the <u>products</u>.

Methane is a <u>compound</u> of carbon and hydrogen. Max asked Izzy to have a go at writing the equation for methane burning in air.

'Be careful Izzy,' he said, 'think about methane being made up of carbon and hydrogen.'

methane + oxygen → carbon dioxide + water

'Well done, Izzy, that's correct. The oxygen reacts with the carbon to form carbon dioxide, and with the hydrogen to form water.'

Izzy knew that this was a chemical reaction because it could not be reversed to make the reactants again (methane and oxygen).

Max showed Izzy an experiment. He placed a nightlight on the table. He then lit the candle and placed a large glass tumbler over it.

'Watch carefully and tell me what happens,' said Max.

Izzy described what she saw; 'The candle is burning brightly. Now it's getting less bright. It's gone out.

'What do you think has happened?' asked Max.

'The candle needed oxygen to burn so all the oxygen must have been used up when the candle went out,' replied Izzy.

An oil rig in the North Sea extracting natural (methane) gas for use in heating and gas cookers

Chemical wordsearch

Find and circle the words in the grid that are listed below. The words can read up, down and diagonally and forwards or backwards.

ACID   CARBON   HYDROGEN   METAL   OXIDE
OXYGEN   PRODUCT   REACTANT   WATER   ZINC

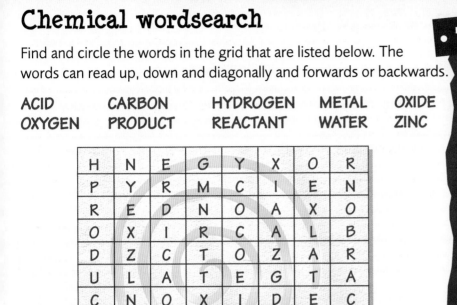

H	N	E	G	Y	X	O	R
P	Y	R	M	C	I	E	N
R	E	D	N	O	A	X	O
O	X	I	R	C	A	L	B
D	Z	C	T	O	Z	A	R
U	L	A	T	E	G	T	A
C	N	O	X	I	D	E	C
T	W	A	T	E	R	M	N

• TOP TIPS •

• When fuels, e.g. coal and gas, burn they form carbon dioxide and water and give out energy.

• Reactants are written on the left-hand side of a word equation.

• Products are written on the right-hand side of a word equation.

A burning question

Containers of different sizes were placed over candles. The time taken for the candles to go out was recorded in the table. Plot a graph of the results and then answer the questions.

Volume (cm³)	Time (s)
125	4
250	7.5
500	15
750	27
1000	30

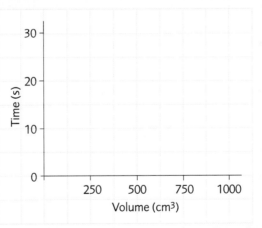

1 What gas is used up when the candle burns in the containers?

....

2 What was the volume of the container that had a leak in it?

....

3 How long would it take before a candle went out in a container with a volume of 375 cm³? ....

DID YOU KNOW?

In 1709, an Act of Parliament banned candle making in your home unless you bought a licence and paid a tax. At this time in British history, light was a form of power, and English state laws controlled the weight, size, production and cost of candles.

Test your knowledge 5

1 The table below gives some information about four substances.

Graphite (carbon)	Insoluble in water. Burns in air to form carbon dioxide, which is soluble in water to give a solution with a pH of 6.
Heptane	Insoluble in water. Burns in air to form carbon dioxide and water.
Potassium	Reacts rapidly with water. Forms a solution with a pH of 11. The gas given off burns with a 'pop'.
Sodium chloride (salt)	Soluble in water. Forms a solution with a pH of 7. Does not burn.

a) Name the gas that burns with a 'pop'. ....

b) A mixture of salt and graphite is to be separated. Explain why warm water is added to the mixture, which is then stirred.

    ....

    ....

c) The mixture of graphite, salt and water is poured through the apparatus shown.

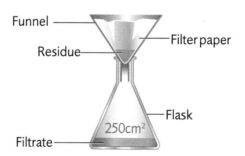

Funnel —

Residue—

Filter paper

Flask

250cm²

Filtrate—

   (i)   Name the residue ....

   (ii) Name the filtrate ....

   (iii) If the filtrate was evaporated to dryness, what would be left?

    ....

d) What information tells you that:

   (i)   potassium is a metal? ....

   (ii) graphite is a non-metal? ....

   (iii) heptane is a compound and NOT an element? ....

    ....

(9 marks)

2 The ingredients in a recipe for American pancakes were:

6 teaspoons baking powder   2 cups of flour   2 tablespoons of sugar
4 tablespoons butter $1^1/_2$ cups of milk
2 eggs   1 teaspoon of salt

a) (i) Which THREE ingredients are obtained from animals?

........................., ... and ....

(ii) Which TWO ingredients are obtained from plants?

.... and ....

(iii) Which ingredient can be extracted from seawater? ....

(iv) Which ingredient is manufactured? ....

b) Here is a conversion table for some measurements.

3 teaspoons = 1 tablespoon
16 tablespoons = 1 cup
2 cups = 1 pint (16 fluid ounces)

(i) How many fluid ounces of milk are there in the American pancakes recipe?

....

(ii) Which TWO measures of the ingredients are the same?

.... and ....

c) The ingredients are mixed to a smooth paste. What has to be done next to convert the smooth paste into American pancakes?

....

....

d) Why is making a pancake an example of a chemical change and not a physical change?

....

e) Write a tick against the changes below that are chemical changes.

A car rusting   ☐
Adding water to citric acid and sodium hydrogencarbonate (baking powder)   ☐
Dissolving salt in water   ☐
Freezing water to make ice   ☐

(15 marks)

(Total 24 marks)

A particular problem

Izzy had been watching a tennis match at Wimbledon on television. That night she had a dream about Wimbledon but it was muddled up with <u>solids</u>, <u>liquids</u> and <u>gases</u>!

In her dream the people in the seats became like a solid. They were arranged in a regular pattern and they could wriggle around in their seats but not leave them.

The people on Wimbledon hill watching the match on the big screen became the liquid. They were packed fairly closely together but the arrangement was random. There were gaps in the crowd and they could move around.

solid   liquid   gas

The three states of matter

On the court, the players, ball boys and ball girls became the gas. They could run freely around and sometimes they ran into and bounced off the barrier surrounding the court!

The next morning, Izzy went to see Max who was under the bonnet of his car.

'What are you doing?' asked Izzy.

'Putting brake fluid into the reservoir,' said Max.

'Why do you use a liquid and not a solid or a gas?' asked Izzy.

'Well,' explained Max, 'if it was a solid and I put my foot on the brake, it wouldn't move. If it was a gas, then it would be compressed. When I put my foot on the brake pedal with liquid in the system, pressure to the brakes travels through the liquid and I stop.'

'Can you smell burnt toast?' said Max as they went indoors. 'Your dad must be trying his hand at cooking again!'

Max explained to Izzy that the tiny particles of burnt toast <u>diffused</u> through the air particles to reach their noses.

Follow the directions

Use the compass directions to follow a trail of cells through the grid. Start in the top-left cell. Shade in each cell as you land on it. If you follow the directions correctly, the shaded cells will spell out a word from this topic.

The first two moves have been done for you, and three others in case you lose your way.

12E	25W	9W	2NE	3SE	5E	3N	3SW	2N	2W	5SE	9W
6N	6SE	5W	2N	4NE	3S	3SE	5N	4SW	2W	1N	3NW
2S	3SE	2E	2N	6E	11W	1S	11E	4W	1N	2NW	2E

A particular question

1 The three states of matter are gas, liquid and ....

2 In which state of matter are particles furthest apart? ....

3 Why is a liquid and not a gas used in the tubes to car brakes?

....

4 Explain why freshly cut grass can be smelt some distance away.

....

• TOP TIPS •

- There are three states of matter: solid, liquid and gas.

- In a solid the particles are arranged in a fixed, close, regular pattern. In a liquid the particles are close together but are able to move freely. In a gas the particles are far apart and they move quickly and randomly.

- The random movement of particles in a gas called diffusion.

A possible solution

Izzy and her dad were on holiday in Malta (an island between the coast of southern Italy and North Africa). Izzy was sitting outside in the sunshine. She was shaking a bottle of Milk of Magnesia so she could take some for her stomach ache. As she shook the bottle the magnesium hydroxide, which is <u>insoluble</u>, formed a <u>suspension</u> with the water.

Her dad came and stood next to her with a running hosepipe.

'Feet up please Izzy,' he said, 'I'm going to wash the sand off the floor with the water.'

Izzy watched how the sand was pushed around the floor by the water jet but did not dissolve; it is insoluble in water.

Laughing, she said to her dad, 'Wouldn't it be great if the sand magically disappeared in the water, then it would be easier to clean.'

'Ahh, ahhh. But remember the saltpans we visited yesterday? Salt is soluble in water so you can't see it. But when the heat from the Sun <u>evaporates</u> the water from the pans, a white deposit of salt is left. The salt doesn't actually 'disappear' when it dissolves (you know that because it tastes salty). Salt is called the <u>solute</u>, and water is called the <u>solvent</u> and together they form a <u>solution</u>.'

Izzy decided to make her own 'saltpan'. She measured out 100 cm³ of water in a measuring jug. She knew this weighed 100 g. She added 4 g of ordinary table salt and stirred the mixture with a spoon (to make it dissolve faster). The salt disappeared. The mixture now weighed 104 g. She put it outside in the Sun to let the water evaporate. When the salt was dry she re-weighed it. It weighed 4 g! She wondered how to get the water back. Her dad had the answer.

Talk about information overload.... I think I need a soluble aspirin.

'If we did this in a lab, we would use a <u>distillation</u> apparatus,' he explained. 'The salt water is heated. The water vapour is passed through a condenser and the water is collected in a beaker.'

'And I guess the water would weigh 100 g!' exclaimed Izzy.

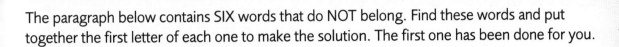

Find the solution

The paragraph below contains SIX words that do NOT belong. Find these words and put together the first letter of each one to make the solution. The first one has been done for you.

To make a solid melt it must be (soluble). By heating the solid you supply the particles of the solid with oxygen. This gives the particles enough light to move apart. If the heat source is removed, the liquid will start to undo and change back to a solid. This is called temperature. When the liquid becomes a solid it transfers its elements to the surroundings.

The part of the solution is the S _ _ _ _ _

Solutions and answers

1   Saline solution contains salt dissolved in water. What is the:

   (i) solute? ....

   (ii) solvent? ....

2   For the following substances write an S if it is soluble in water, and write an I if it is insoluble in water.

   sand ....   chalk ....   wood ....   oxygen ....

   salt ....   sugar ....   copper ....   flour ....

3   You are asked to dissolve a lump of sugar in some water. State THREE things you could do to increase the rate at which the sugar dissolves.

   (i)   ....

   (ii) ....

   (iii) ....

DID YOU KNOW?

'Salary' gets its name from the Latin word 'salarium', which was the term used for a soldier's pay in the army of ancient Rome. The pay included a large ration of salt. In Roman times this was a substance of high value and was used for exchanges with other goods.

• TOP TIPS •

• A solute is the name given to a substance that dissolves in a solvent.

• A solvent is the name given to the liquid that dissolves a solute.

• A solution is a mixture of a solvent and a solute.

Cheque it out

Izzy's dad was very agitated. He had just received his bank statement, which showed that, mysteriously, £60 had been taken out of his account. He immediately informed his bank about the matter on the phone. A few days later the bank contacted him to say that the cheque for £60 had been found and the signature had obviously been forged. It was now a matter for the police.

After a couple of weeks the police rang Izzy's dad.

'We've found the culprit,' the policeman said, 'It's your old friend Mr C Rook.'

'How did you manage to find him?' asked Izzy's dad.

'<u>Chromatography</u>' came the proud reply, 'I'll send you a copy of the report.'

REPORT
Stolen Cheque

Our forensic expert, Mr I C Hall, asked us to collect pens from the various suspects, which we did. Using chromatography he managed to match the ink in Mr Rook's pen to the ink on the cheque. Below is a copy of Mr Hall's results.

When challenged Mr Rook admitted to the crime.

Special note:
Mr Hall said that Izzy could try chromatography using filter paper or blotting paper and some coloured pens or coloured sweets. Here is a diagram to show her how.

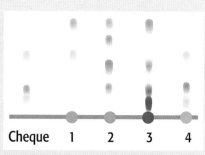

Cheque   1   2   3   4

Number 4 was the ink from Mr Rook's pen. It matches the results obtained from Izzy's dad's ink on the cheque

Filter paper — Black ink spot

Water

Using the method described in the note, Izzy carried out a chromatography experiment with the ink from her water-soluble black pen. After an hour the filter paper looked like this.

She thought that the turquoise ink must be more soluble than the yellow ink. Max thought the yellow ink stuck more to the paper than the turquoise ink. They were both correct!

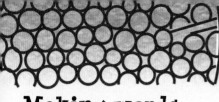

Making words

Using any of the letters from the word 'CHROMATOGRAPHY', answer the clues below. The number in brackets after a clue tells you the number of letters in the word(s).

The first one has been done for you.

1 It anchors a plant to the soil. (4) R O O T

2 Spotless often chases one in the garden. (3) _ _ _

3 The young of this animal are called kids. (4) _ _ _ _

4 The light from this helps you see in the dark. (5) _ _ _ _ _

5 It is used with a pestle in the laboratory. (6) _ _ _ _ _ _

6 An orange root vegetable. (6) _ _ _ _ _ _

7 Max drives one. (5, 3) _ _ _ _ _ _ _ _

• TOP TIPS •

- Chromatography is a method used to separate mixtures dissolved in a solvent.

- The solvent used in chromatography must not react with the substances being tested.

What's in a colour?

To find out what colours are present in a black sweet a little of it was dissolved in water and a few drops of it were put on a filter paper. Spots of red, blue, green and orange food dyes were also put on the filter paper. Here are the results.

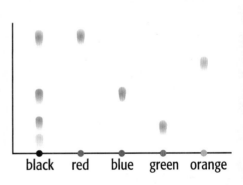

black red blue green orange

a) How many different coloured food dyes are there in the black dye? ....

b) Which three colours must be present in the black dye?

....

c) Which coloured dye was NOT in the black dye?

....

d) Give a reason, other than its colour, which shows that the dye named in c) above was NOT present in the black dye.

....

DID YOU KNOW?

Chromatography is one of the tests used to detect illegal substances in athlete's urine. Urine samples are tested against known illegal drugs. The method can detect the presence of less than 0.000000000001 g of an illegal substance.

A burning issue

Izzy's house did not have central heating. They used coal fires and electric fires to keep the house warm in winter. It costs a lot of money to keep a house warm. So that heat was not lost Izzy's dad had the loft <u>insulated</u> and the windows double-glazed. (He had to let some air in so that the fires burnt safely.) He was always telling Izzy off for leaving on lights unnecessarily.

'You're wasting energy,' he would say to her, 'Go and use some of your energy and turn out the lights in your room.'

Energy makes people and machines work.

That evening Izzy and her dad were sitting in front of the open coal fire after supper. Izzy could just make out the silhouettes of the bare trees against the wintery sky through the window. She looked at the fire and thought how it was part of an energy chain: the growing tree outside took energy from the Sun to make building blocks so that it could grow. Eventually the tree would die and be buried and after millions of years be mined as coal and all that stored energy would be released as heat when it was burnt. She imagined how the Earth would have been millions of years ago. Dinosaurs used to live in the forests where giant fern plants and trees grew.

When the trees died they were pressed and heated and turned into coal. In the North Sea crustaceans and plants flourished. When they died they were covered by sand and mud and slowly changed into oil and gas. Petrol and diesel can be obtained from oil.

All these fuels are called <u>fossil fuels</u> and are used to provide energy. Izzy knew that most of the coal mined is used in power stations to generate electricity. Fossil fuels are non-renewable, which means that they will run out. They also cause pollution, e.g. smoke, ash and waste gases.

Izzy thought about where energy would come from when non-renewable fuels had run out. Trees could be felled and burnt – that is a <u>renewable fuel</u> – but the world would have to grow thousands of vast forests. Instead, other renewable energy sources, which are much cleaner, are being developed.

Examples are: wind energy harnessed by wind farms; water energy harnessed by hydroelectric power stations and from the waves and tides; geothermal energy harnessed in New Zealand by using hot rocks to heat water; energy from the Sun converted into electricity by solar panels.

A wind farm

Name game

Write the answers to the clues in the boxes. Write the letters from the SHADED boxes to spell a well-known scientific word.

- The name given to fuels that are being used up and cannot be replaced.

			—								

- It is produced, together with carbon dioxide when a fuel burns.

- The study of rocks.

The word is:

Warming up

Using only the words below complete the following sentences.
Each word may be used only once.

FUEL	HEAT	RENEWABLE	SOLAR	WAVES

1   A .... is a substance that burns in air to produce heat energy.

2   We use energy to light and .... the places where we live and work.

3   .... cells are used to convert energy from the Sun into electricity.

4   A .... energy resource is one that will not run out during the lifetime of the Earth.

5   Energy from the sea can be obtained from .... and tides.

• TOP TIPS •

- **Coal, gas and oil are fossil fuels. They are non-renewable sources of energy.**

- **Burning fossil fuels pollutes the atmosphere.**

- **Wood, wind, Sun, waves and tides are renewable sources of energy.**

Test your knowledge 6

1 An experiment to see how the temperature of ice taken from the freezer changed when it was left in the kitchen was set up as follows.

A thermometer was put in a plastic cup full of crushed ice, which was placed in the freezer. After an hour the cup was removed from the freezer and the temperature was recorded every five minutes.

Temperature (°C)	−10	0	0	0	0	3	7	12	18	22	24	25	25
Time (min)		0	5	10	15	20	25	30	35	40	45	50	55	60

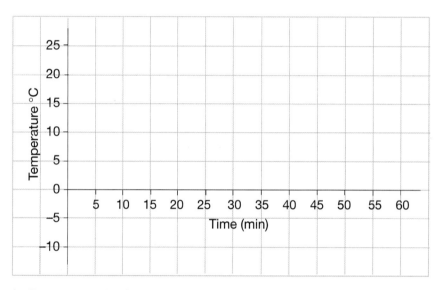

a) Draw a graph showing how the temperature of the ice changed over time.

b) (i) What was the temperature inside the freezer? .... °C

   (ii) What was the temperature of the kitchen? ....°C

c) There are three states:

   A: particles move about randomly, occasionally colliding with one another
   B: particles move past each other and are close together
   C: particles vibrate about fixed points

   Using the letters A, B and C, how were the particles arranged:

   (i) in the freezer? ....

   (ii) at 25 °C? ....

d) Ice floats on water. What did this tell you about:

   (i) the density of ice compared with the density of water?

   ....

(ii) distances between the molecules of water. Put a tick in the box beside the correct statement.

The molecules are further apart in ice than in water. ☐

The molecules are further apart in water than in ice. ☐

The molecules are the same distance apart in ice and water. ☐

(10 marks)

2   The pie chart shows the energy used by the World.

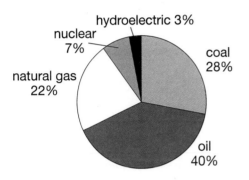

a)   What percentage of the World's energy is supplied by fossil fuels?

....

b)   Give TWO types of energy that can be obtained from fossil fuels.

(i)   ....

(ii) ....

c)   Why are fossil fuels described as non-renewable energy resources?

....

....

Based on current projections, within approximately 75 years, the world will have used up all of its extractable:

- coal
- oil
- natural gas
- uraninum-235 (a source of nuclear energy).

Not enough wind power and hydroelectric power can be harnessed to make much difference and both involve major environmental cost.

d)   What will be the major source of the World's energy in 80 years time?

....

(6 marks)

(Total 16 marks)

Circuit training

'What are you doing?' Izzy asked Max.

'Making a doll's house for my niece,' he replied. 'I'm about to put in the lighting <u>electrical</u> <u>circuit</u>.'

'Can I help?' asked Izzy.

'Yes, of course. I want to have lights in each room of the doll's house and one in the roof space, here,' answered Max. 'Using symbols we can draw a <u>circuit</u> <u>diagram</u> to represent the way in which the lights and wire are connected.'

He then drew a circuit diagram on a piece of paper to show the lighting in the doll's house. He labelled the symbols so that Izzy could use them in circuit diagrams of her own.

'What is a <u>cell</u>?' asked Izzy.

'It's the electricity source; I'm using a torch battery. The long line in the cell symbol represents the positive terminal and the short line represents the negative terminal,' explained Max.

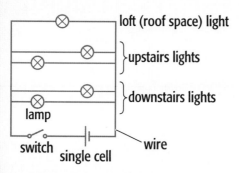
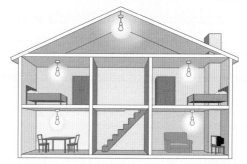

Izzy studied Max's drawing of the circuit diagram. She then drew her own circuit diagram to show a different way of connecting the lamps in the circuit for the doll's house. It is shown below.

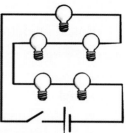

'Ahhh,' said Max. 'You have drawn a <u>series</u> <u>circuit</u>. Mine is a <u>parallel</u> <u>circuit</u>. If you put the switch down in your circuit, all the lights would go on. If one of the lights 'blows' (goes out because the filament in the bulb breaks), all the lights will go out and the circuit will be broken. <u>Current</u> can't flow in a broken circuit. However, in my circuit, if one of the lights blows the other four will stay on. The current can still find a way to flow through the unbroken circuit.'

'Then the lights for our Christmas tree must be in series,' said Izzy. 'If one of the lights goes out then they all go out. Is our house wired like the doll's house?'

'It is very similar,' answered Max. 'Except it has two parallel circuits; one for the room lights and the other for the power circuit. There is also a different circuit for the electric oven.'

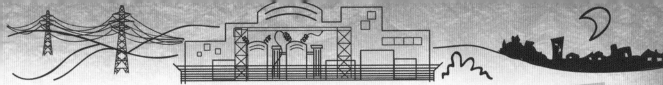

Connecting up

Join one group of letters from Group A with one group of letters from Group B to make ten words about electricity.

The first one has been done for you.

Group A				
CE	CIR	ELECT	LA	PARA
POSI	SER	SWI	TERM	WI

Group B				
CUIT	IES	INAL	LL	LLEL
MP	RE	RICITY	TCH	TIVE

The ten words are:

CELL

Circuit skill

1   Name three appliances in your house that use electricity.

(i) ....

(ii) ....

(iii) ....

2   Draw a circuit consisting of a switch, a cell, connecting wire and three bulbs. The circuit must contain bulbs in series or in parallel.

3   Copy the parallel circuit for the lights in the doll's house but include switches so that each light can be turned 'on' and 'off' independently.

· TOP TIPS ·

- An electrical circuit must be complete before a current can flow.

- There are two types of electrical circuit: series and parallel.

- A battery (or cell) has a positive and a negative terminal.

DID YOU KNOW?

If the energy from a hurricane blowing for just one day could be harnessed and converted into electricity, there would be enough to keep the whole of America supplied for up to three years.

Lighting up

Izzy's dad was sitting by the fire late in the evening, drinking a glass of wine and reading a book with Spotless curled up at his feet. Suddenly all the lights went out. The room wasn't very dark because the fire gave out light. Some minutes later the lights came on again. Max came in with a torch.

'The downstairs <u>fuse</u> had blown. I've switched it back on.'

Next morning when Izzy came down for breakfast, Max and her dad were discussing the electrics in the house. Max told her a fuse had blown in the night and the downstairs lights had gone off.

'It was easy to fix. Last year the house was fitted with mini-circuit breakers (mcbs). All I had to do was flick a switch.'

What did the lightbulb say to the fuse?

That's a blow!

Izzy asked him to show her the circuit box for the house. There were five separate circuits in the house: two lighting circuits (one upstairs and one downstairs); two power circuits (again upstairs and downstairs), and one for the cooker circuit. Each circuit could carry a different amount of current. Max explained that lighting circuits can carry up to 5 <u>amperes</u> <u>(amps)</u>, power circuits can carry 13 amps and the cooker circuit 30 amps. If the current going through the circuits went over these values the mcb was tripped.

This is a safety feature built-in to all house circuits. It prevents a fire breaking out when a household appliance, e.g. a kettle overheats due to a fault that causes too much current to flow in the circuit.

Max was on a roll now and quickly made a sketch on a piece of paper.

'Imagine a man pushing a wheelbarrow over rough ground,' he said. 'The force pushing the wheelbarrow is the <u>voltage</u> (measured in volts). The load in the wheelbarrow is the amount of current (measured in amperes). The larger the load, the greater the voltage required to move it. The rough ground is the resistance (measured in ohms). The rougher the ground (the greater the resistance), the greater the voltage required to move it.

In an electric circuit, the thicker the wire (i.e. the smaller the resistance) the more easily current can flow through it. The supply of electricity to a house is at a constant (same) voltage (230 volts). In order to vary the amount of current in a house, wires of different thicknesses are used.'

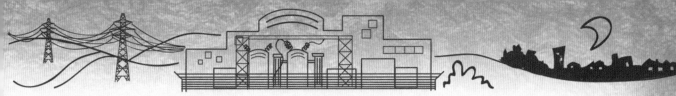

Current scrabble

Write the words below vertically in the grid.

The first one has been done for you.

CURRENT   FUSE   LAMP   OHM   PARALLEL   SERIES

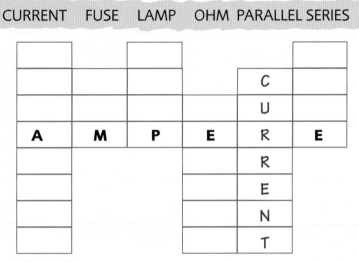

The grid spells out horizontally: **A M P E R E** with **CURRENT** running vertically through the R.

Current knowledge

1   What are the units of:

(i)   current? ....

(ii)   voltage? ....

(iii) resistance? ....

2   Your house is properly wired. There is a fault in your kettle. What should happen to prevent current flowing through the kettle?

    ....

3   You have a circuit of a cell, lamp and switch connected by a piece of copper wire. Would the current in the circuit increase or decrease if the copper wire was stretched to make it longer and thinner?

    ....

Can you resist it?

Izzy's torch wasn't working so she took it to Max and asked him to have a look at it. She had kept the instructions, which included a diagram.

Max suggested she checked the following.

1 Are the batteries put in correctly?
2 Are the batteries charged?
3 Has the bulb 'blown'?
4 Is there a break in the wire?
5 Does the switch work?

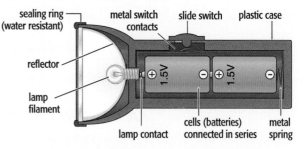

Izzy checked her torch. The positive (+) terminal (end) of one battery was connected correctly to the negative (−) terminal (end) of the other battery. Max found an electrical test meter in the garage and tested the voltage of each of the batteries. They both measured 1.5 V.

'They're OK,' said Max.

Next Izzy unscrewed the bulb from the torch. Max used the circuit test setting to see if any current was passing through it. There was no reading.

'There's your problem,' said Max. 'The filament inside the bulb has broken.'

'When Izzy looked carefully at the very thin wire stretched inside the bulb she could see the break. She screwed a new bulb in and the torch worked.

'Can we test the batteries I keep as spares for my radio, CD player and iPod?' asked Izzy.

Max tested all Izzy's spare batteries. She had some at 1.5 V, and others at 4.5 V and several at 9 V. One or two had measured zero and they put these to one side to be recycled.

'We've tested the voltage in a circuit,' said Izzy, 'but how do you test how much current there is?'

'You use an ammeter,' said Max. 'I've got one in the garage. Come and have a look.'

Max showed Izzy that the more bulbs that were joined in series in a circuit, the smaller the current is through the circuit. Increasing the number of bulbs increases the <u>resistance</u> in the circuit and the bulbs are less bright. He also showed her that when more batteries are used in the circuit, the current increases.

How does the dimmer switch on my bedroom light work?' asked Izzy.

Max drew another of his circuit diagrams.

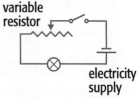

'When you click the switch on it connects the circuit and your light comes on. Turning the switch further varies the resistance in the circuit. More or less current can flow and this alters the brightness of the light.'

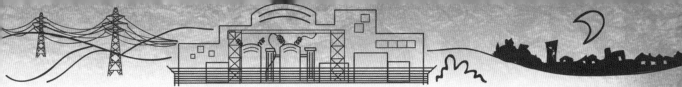

Find the power driver

Find the word connected with electricity by crossing out the letters that appear three times in the grid below.

V	P	G	B	L	A
H	T	O	U	H	O
T	H	M	E	R	P
G	L	F	V	F	I
M	U	L	E	U	M
O	P	S	F	V	G

The word is _ _ _ _ _ _ _ _ _ _

> ## • TOP TIPS •
>
> • **A battery (cell) is a source of energy in an electric circuit.**
>
> • **The amount of current in a circuit is measured by an ammeter.**
>
> • **A resistor varies the amount of current that flows in a circuit.**

What's wrong?

In each of the circuits below there are two switches (S1 and S2) and three bulbs (A, B and C). For each of the circuits write down the letter of the bulb(s) that will light. If no bulb will light write 'none'.

1 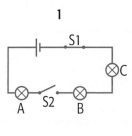 **2** 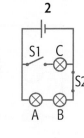 **3** 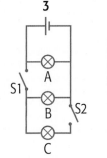 **4**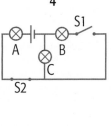

DID YOU KNOW?

The supply of electricity has to be carefully monitored. Electricity is used up the instant it is made. During peak periods of demand such as Christmas Day, more electricity has to be produced.

Test your knowledge 7

1 A circuit is set up as shown below.

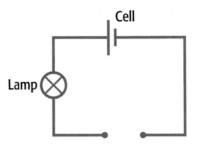

The switch is broken. Put a tick by the object that could be used to replace the switch and complete the circuit so the bulb lights.

another bulb ☐ plastic biro ☐ steel paper clip ☐

pencil lead ☐ silver spoon ☐ another cell ☐

(5 marks)

2 A circuit was set up to be like traffic lights.

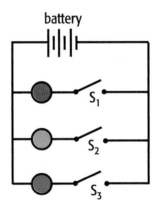

a) Which switches must be closed in order to make the following lights go on?

(i) red ....

(ii) red and amber ....

(iii) green ....

(iv) amber ....

b) If all the switches were closed and the bulb in the amber light was removed, which lights would go on, if any?

....

(6 marks)

3 Christmas tree lights can be bought in two types shown in the following diagrams.

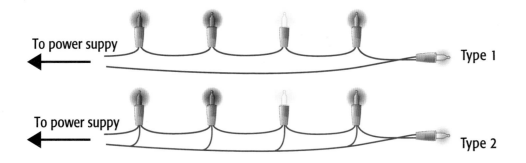

a) Using  ⊗ to represent a bulb and ⊣⊢ to represent the power supply, draw circuit diagrams for both the Christmas tree lights circuits shown above.

Type 1:

Type 2:

b) What advantage does the Type 2 circuit have over the Type 1 circuit?

....

....

c) Explain why, when extra bulbs are added to the Type 1 circuit, the light from the bulbs fades.

....

....

(10 marks)

(Total 21 marks)

Don't force it!

Izzy sometimes baby-sat for a friend in the village. She often pushed the baby in her pram. She walked down the hill into the High Street and on the way home she went back up the hill. She found that it was easier to pull the pram up the hill rather than push it. Force, she thought, is either a 'push' or a 'pull'. She could alter the speed at which she pushed the pram, and to turn a corner, she pushed the pram at a different angle.

When she got home Izzy sat down in the armchair in front of the TV. The cushion sank beneath her.

'What forces are here?' she wondered. 'Since I'm not moving, the forces must be equal.'

There are only two forces to balance she reasoned. The force of her weight going down must equal the force from the springs and cushion going up.

That gave Izzy an idea. She found Spotless's plastic ball and went to the kitchen. She filled the sink with water and put the plastic ball in the water. It floated. The upward force of the water equalled the downward force (weight) of the ball.

'When I was younger,' she remembered, 'I wore armbands to keep me afloat when I was learning to swim.' The deeper she pushed the ball in the water, the bigger the upward push of the water.

In order to understand how a force is acting, its size and its direction must be known. In the pictures below an arrow is used to represent the force; the larger the arrow, the larger the force and its direction shows the direction of the force.

The two forces are equal. The pram is stationary.

Izzy's pull is greater than the force pulling the pram down the hill. The pram goes up the hill.

The pull of the pram down the hill is greater than Izzy's pull. The pram goes down the hill.

Izzy realised that there was another force acting on the pram, called friction. There are friction forces between the wheels of the pram and the path. Friction is a force that acts against the movement of an object to slow things down.

Clockword

In each case write down the letters of the hour hand followed by the letters of the minute hand to make words used in this unit.

The first one has been done for you.

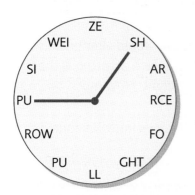

1 Quarter to one .... **PUSH**

2 Half-past seven ....

3 Ten o'clock ....

4 Quarter-past four ....

5 Twenty-to-two ....

6 Twenty-five past eleven ....

A moving question

The following pictures show forces acting. Draw arrows to show the direction of the forces. For each action increase the thickness of the arrow to show the larger force.

DID YOU KNOW?

Fish have an air-filled sack in their bodies called a swim bladder. The fish can control how much air goes in and out of the swim bladder. When more air is let in the buoyancy (ability to float), increases. This is how a fish stays buoyant as the pressure of the water increases with depth.

A dense topic

'Dad, is it true that I would weigh less on the Moon?' asked Izzy. 'We saw an old film today of the first men on the Moon. They were able to do somersaults, even with large packs on their backs.'

Her dad answered, 'Your <u>mass</u> would stay the same, but your weight would alter because weight depends on <u>gravity</u>. Gravity is a force between two masses which acts to pull them together. It is this force between you and the Earth that is called weight. How much do you weigh Izzy?' asked her dad.

'About 54 kilograms (kg),' answered Izzy.

'Well, no,' said her dad. 'That's your mass. Your mass would be 54 kg wherever you went in the Universe but your weight would change. Mass is a measure of the amount of material. Weight depends on gravity. On Earth the gravitational pull is 10 kg per <u>Newton</u> (N), so you would weigh 540 Newtons on Earth. On the Moon you would weigh only 81 Newtons, but on Jupiter you would weigh a massive 1350 Newtons. And in Space your weight would be zero. So yes, you would weigh less on the Moon, but your mass would stay the same.'

'Wasn't Newton the man who had an apple fall on his head which gave him the idea of gravity?' asked Izzy.

'Yes,' said her dad. 'Weight is measured using a forcemeter (sometimes called a Newtonmeter). On bathroom scales the dial is altered to make it read in kilograms and not in Newtons.'

'How about water?' asked Izzy. 'Do I weigh less when I'm swimming in a pool?'

'You do,' said her dad. 'And you would weigh even less in the Dead Sea because the salt in it makes it denser than swimming pool water. In fact I've seen photographs of people floating in the Dead Sea reading newspapers. The <u>density</u> of an object is its mass divided by its volume.

$$\text{Density} = \frac{\text{mass}}{\text{volume}}$$

Since mass is measured in grams or kilograms, and volume in cubic centimetres (cc or cm^3) or cubic metres (m^3), the units of density are either grams per cm^3 or kilograms per m^3.'

Text messaging

The diagram shows the numbers on a mobile phone. Use the numbers to work out the words associated with mass, weight and density. Some of the letters have been done for you already.

The first one has been done for you.

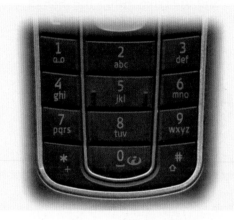

1 4728489 GRAVITY

2 6277 _ _ _ S

3 6666 _ O _ N

4 32784 _ _ _ T _

5 639866 N _ _ _ _ _

6 934448 _ _ _ G _ _

7 3367489 _ _ _ _ _ T _

8 36723 _ _ _ C _

9 54564726 _ _ _ O _ _ _ _

10 865863 _ _ _ _ _ E

DID YOU KNOW?

Osmium is the densest known metal. Its density is 22.6 g per cm^3. A piece of osmium the size of an orange would have a mass of 4.5 kg!

Density questions

1 Draw a circle around the objects below that float in water.

apple bicycle cork glass pebble plastic ball osmium silver spoon

2 Suggest why airship balloons are filled with helium gas and not with carbon dioxide.

....

3 What is the density of a piece of metal that has a mass of 12 g and a volume of 3 cm^3?

....

• TOP TIPS •

- **Mass is the amount of matter in a substance. Mass is measured in kilograms (kg).**
- **Weight is a force caused by gravity. Weight is measured in Newtons (N).**

  Gravity of the earth = 10 kg/N
  On Earth: weight = mass x 10
- **Objects that are less dense than water float. Objects that are denser than water sink.**

Friction forces

'Dad, we've got a question on friction for homework. I know that friction is a force that acts in the opposite way to the direction in which things are moving. We've been asked to give examples of helpful friction forces and unhelpful friction forces. When riding a bicycle the friction forces between the tyres and the road allow the bike to go forwards. When the brakes are applied the friction between the brake blocks and the tyres brings the bike to a halt. But I'm stuck for more examples. Can you think of any?'

'Well,' said her dad. 'Friction forces between your trainers and the path stop you from sliding. Friction lets us strike matches on matchboxes and rubbing two sticks together produces heat in the form of a spark used to light a fire. Friction keeps knots in ropes from untying and potters shape pots by making use of the friction between their hands and clay.'

'Examples of friction forces being unhelpful are that they make it difficult to drag large objects. Remember the trouble Max and I had when we tried to drag a cupboard in your room? Friction forces cause heat and can damage moving parts in machinery.'

'When you went skiing with your school last year, some of your friends waxed the bottom of their skis to reduce the friction between the skis and the snow so that they went even faster. Oiling the joints on moving parts has the same effect. By reducing the friction forces, overheating is prevented and wear and tear on the moving parts is reduced. A reduction in friction forces can be dangerous. When Max had his minor car accident he skidded on the wet surface of the road.'

A not so slippery problem

My first is in FORCE but not in PRESSURE.

My second's in ROTATION and also in RESISTANCE.

My third's in CLOCKWISE but not in SEE-SAW.

My fourth's not in PIVOT but is in FULCRUM.

My fifth's not in SPEED but is in RATE.

My sixth's in LINEAR and also in TIME.

My seventh's in MOTION but not in DISTANCE.

My eighth's not in METRES but is in NEWTONS.

My whole is a force that tries to prevent motion.

The word is _ _ _ _ _ _ _ _

A forceful experiment

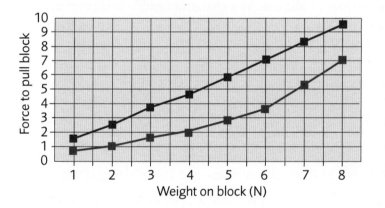

A block with different weights on it was pulled across a rough surface using a forcemeter. The graph of force (measured in Newtons) was plotted against the weight of the block (measured in Newtons).

The experiment was performed:
a) when the block was dry
b) when the block was wet.

1   Which line represents the results when the block was dry? ....

2   What TWO conclusions can you make from the red line?

....

....

DID YOU KNOW?

The Earth has been spinning ever since it was formed thousands of millions of years ago. It does not need a force to keep it going because there is very little friction in space to stop it. The Earth is said to be in 'perpetual (everlasting) motion'.

Test your knowledge 8

1 a) Use some of the words below to complete the passage. A word may be used only once or not at all.

constant	direction	Earth	friction
gravity	large	move	Newton
push	size	stationary	weight

A force is a .... or a pull. It can be in any .... The .... of an

object is the pull downwards exerted by the .... on the object. We call this

particular kind of pull the force of ....

A force also has .... If there are two equal forces pushing on the same

object, the object remains ....

If a force is applied to an object and there is no opposing force then the object will

....

b) A ball is thrown from one person to another in a game of catch. The diagram shows the path of the ball.

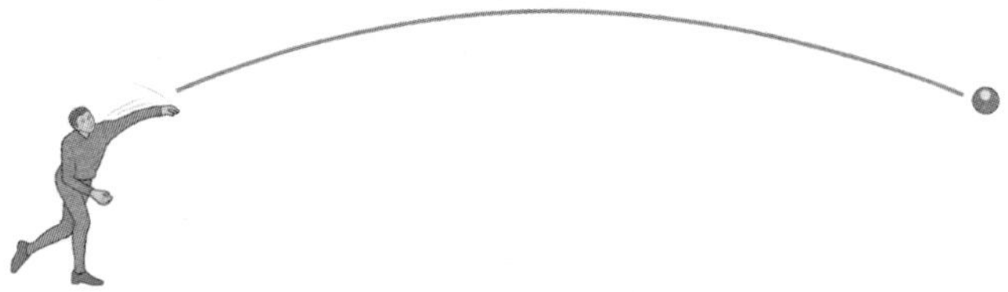

How can you tell from the path of the ball that there is a force acting on it?

....

....

c) Using arrows show the SIZE and DIRECTION of forces acting on each of the following.

(i)

Book resting on a table

(ii)

Ball being dropped

(iii)

Car starting to move

(16 marks)

2 a) What are the units of:

   (i) mass? ....

   (ii) weight? ....

b) Why is gravity less on the Moon than on Earth?

   ....

   ....

c) (i) Name the force that helps objects such as cars to start moving and to stop.

   ....

   (ii) Suggest why a motorist should leave a greater distance from the car in front
        when the road is wet.

   ....

   ....

(7 marks)

3 Submarines can move up, down, backwards or forwards. They are able to do this by
changing the direction and size of forces. The diagrams below show the size and
direction of these forces. Complete the table to show the direction of the submarine.

The first one has been done for you.

	Submarine moves			
	up	down	forwards	backwards
Back Front		✓	✓	
Back Front				
c Back Front				
Back Front				

(4 marks)

(Total 27 marks)

Worlds apart

It was 9 am. 'I'm going to phone Penny,' Izzy said to Max. 'I need to talk to her about her coming over from America to stay with us next month.'

'You'll have to wait,' said Max. 'It's 4 am where she lives and she'll still be in bed.'

'Can you please explain time zones and also, can you tell me about the phases of the Moon and eclipses?' asked Izzy.

Max used diagrams and while he was talking Izzy took notes. She made a 'smart mobile' for her bedroom by keying her notes on to the computer, printing them out and then sticking them on to a square of cardboard with Max's drawings. She used a luminous pen to colour in his drawings so they showed up in the dark. Izzy and Max also cut some photographs out of one of her dad's old science journals and stuck these on too.

Day and night

The Earth spins on its axis – it takes 24 hours to complete one turn. It turns so slowly and smoothly, we don't feel it moving. The Earth is also travelling around the Sun; it takes 365 days to make a complete turn around the Sun. In the diagram the Sun is shining on half of the Earth; this side will be daytime. On the other half of the Earth it will be dark; it will be night-time. As the Earth rotates some places become light while others become dark.

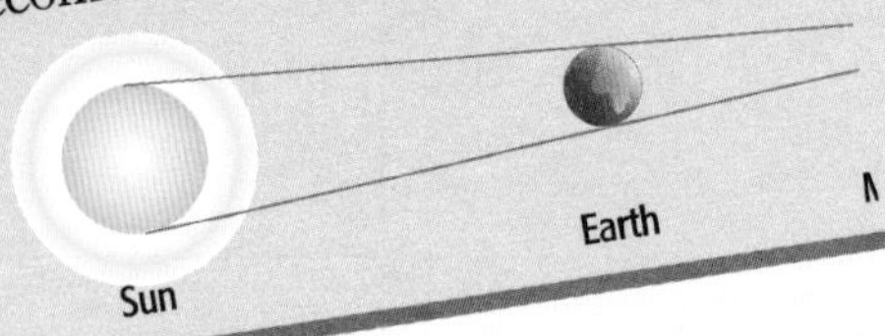

Sun   Earth   ∧

Phases of the Moon

The Moon rotates around the Earth. The different views of the Moon are called its phases, e.g. full Moon, first quarter, new Moon and second quarter.

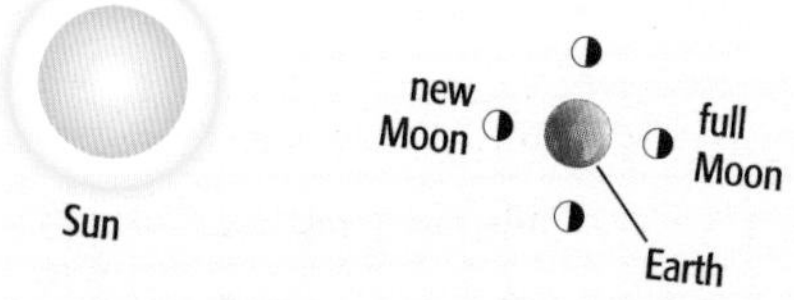

Sun   new Moon   full Moon   Earth

When astronauts first landed on the Moon, they saw that the Earth gave similar patterns to the Moon.

Eclipse of the Sun

An eclipse of the Sun occurs when the Sun, Moon and Earth are in a line. The Moon blocks the light from the Sun. An eclipse of the Moon occurs when the Sun, Earth and Moon are in line. The Earth blocks the light from the Sun. Because the Earth is larger than the Moon, an eclipse of the Moon occurs more often than an eclipse of the Sun.

Space fillers

Use the clues to fill in the missing letters. All the completed words are objects in the Solar System.

- A daisy-like flower.
- A narrow road.
- Izzy might say this to Spotless to make him move towards her.
- To let somebody know something.
- Sound made by a cow.
- 'RAT' backwards.

_ _ _ _ _ _ OID
P _ _ _ _ T
_ _ _ _ T
SA _ _ _ _ ITE
_ _ _ N
S _ _ _

1   Circle the correct description of what causes an eclipse of the Moon.

The Sun casts a shadow of the Moon on the Earth.
The Sun casts a shadow of the Earth on the Moon.
The Earth casts a shadow of the Moon on the Sun.
The Earth casts a shadow of the Sun on the Moon.

2   How long does it take for the Moon to orbit the Earth once? ....

3   Why does the Moon appear to shine at night?
    ....
    ....

4   a) We always see the same side of the Moon. What does this tell you about the time taken for the Moon to spin once on its axis and the time it takes for the Moon to complete one orbit of the Earth?
       ....

    b) How do we know what the far side of the Moon looks like?
       ....

The final frontier

On a clear night Izzy loved lying in bed and looking through her window at the stars, the Moon and the planets, e.g. Mars and Jupiter. Stars are much larger than planets. They are like our Sun; they give out their own light. They are said to be <u>luminous</u>. The planets reflect light. They are <u>non-luminous</u>. That's why stars twinkle and planets do not. The Sun is very large and it is much nearer Earth than the other stars. It's so bright during the day that we're unable to see the stars. The Moon can sometimes be seen because it acts like a mirror and reflects light from the Sun. One thing puzzled Izzy,

'Why do stars move?'

Max had the answer the following morning.

'The stars don't move, said Max. They appear to move because the Earth rotates. 'It's similar to when you are sitting in a train and the train on the next platform moves. It feels like your train is moving.

'Max, how can I remember the names and positions of all the planets?' asked Izzy.

'When I was at school,' said Max 'we were taught the following mnemonic.'

My Very Educated Mother Just Showed Us Nine Planets
(Mercury, Venus, Earth, Mars, Jupiter, Saturn, Uranus, Neptune and Pluto)

Pluto
Neptune
Uranus
Saturn
Mars
Jupiter
Venus
Earth
Mercury
Sun

'Between Mars and Jupiter' continued Max, 'there is the asteroid belt. It is thought to be matter that did not come together to form a planet. Each planet is kept in its orbit by <u>gravity</u>. The large mass of the Sun pulls the planets towards it as they revolve around the Sun. There are also comets and meteors in our Solar System.'

Izzy asked, 'What makes our seasons.'

Max said, 'The Earth is tilted. When the northern hemisphere is tilted towards the Sun, it will be closer to the Sun than the southern hemisphere. The northern hemisphere will receive warmer weather and longer days; it is summer. In the southern hemisphere it is winter because it is tilted away from the Sun. When the northern hemisphere is tilted away from the Sun, it is further from the Sun. It will have colder weather and shorter days; it is winter. In the southern hemisphere it is summer because it is tilted toward the Sun.'

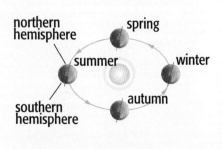

northern hemisphere
spring
summer
winter
autumn
southern hemisphere

'So next Christmas, when dad and I are in New Zealand, it will be summer and we can have Christmas lunch on the beach!' replied Izzy.

Spaced out!

Arrange the planet names listed below to fit the grid. Discover the shaded word – it has everything in it – matter, energy and Space. The first planet has been put in for you.

EARTH   JUPITER   MARS   MERCURY   NEPTUNE   SATURN   URANUS   VENUS

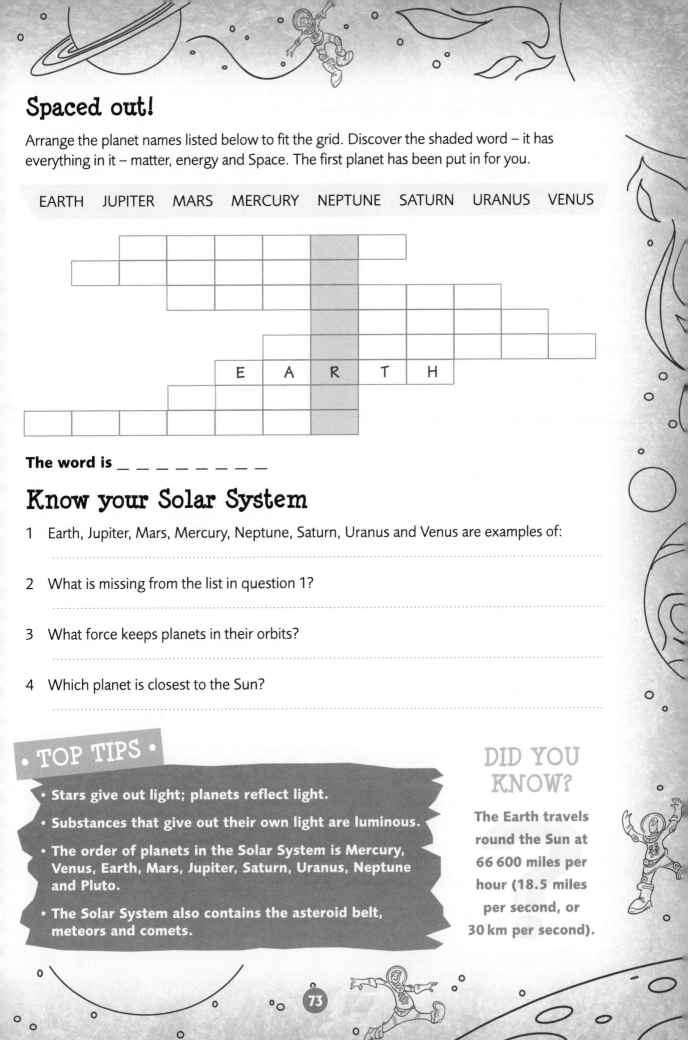

The word is _ _ _ _ _ _ _ _

Know your Solar System

1   Earth, Jupiter, Mars, Mercury, Neptune, Saturn, Uranus and Venus are examples of:

   ....

2   What is missing from the list in question 1?

   ....

3   What force keeps planets in their orbits?

   ....

4   Which planet is closest to the Sun?

   ....

Test your knowledge 9

1 The diagram below shows the orbits of Venus, Earth and Jupiter. (The planets are not drawn to scale.)

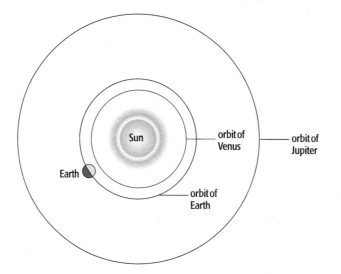

a) On the above diagram draw the orbits of:

   (i) Mercury (label this 'orbit X')
   (ii) Mars (label this 'orbit Y').

   Some of the planets in the Solar System can be seen from Earth.

b) Why can the planets be seen at night?

   ....

c) (i) When seen from Earth why does the size of Venus vary?

   ....

   ....

   (ii) Mark with a V on the diagram above, the position where Venus appears to be at its largest.

d) (i) Mark with a J on the diagram above the position of Jupiter where it appears brightest.

   (ii) Explain why it appears to be brighter at this position.

   ....

   ....

e) Suggest why half the Earth is shaded in the diagram above.

   ....

   ....

(12 marks)

2 The photographs below show two phases of the Moon and the dates of these phases.

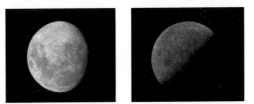

[a] Full Moon, December 15 [b] Last quarter Moon, December 23

a) When in December was there:

(i) a new Moon? ....

(ii) the first quarter Moon? ....

b) (i) How many days does it take for the Earth to complete one orbit of the Sun?

....

(ii) Why are there 13 lunar months in a year?

....

....

c) Look at these dates: 21 March   21 June   21 September   21 December

After which date do the hours of daylight become longer than the hours of darkness (night-time)?

....

d) (i) Draw a diagram to show an eclipse of the Moon as seen from Earth.

(ii) Draw a diagram to show a total eclipse of the Sun as seen from the Moon.

(iii) Why does an eclipse of the Sun as seen from the Moon, last longer than an eclipse of the Sun as seen from Earth?

....

....

e) When there is a total eclipse of the Sun as seen from Earth, which of the following statements is correct? Put a tick in the box against the correct answer.

☐ There is a new Moon   ☐ The Moon is in its first quarter

☐ There is a full Moon   ☐ The Moon is in its last quarter

(14 marks)

(Total 26 marks)

Glossary

Acid Substance that dissolves in water to give a solution with a pH less than 7.

Adolescence A stage in human development where there is a great change in emotional and physical development.

Alkali Base that dissolves in water to give a solution with a pH greater than 7.

Ammeter Instrument used to measure current.

Amperes (amps) Unit of measurement of current.

Amphibian Vertebrates that can live in and out of water, e.g. frog.

Antacid Substance that neutralises excess acid in the stomach.

Base Substance that reacts with an acid to form a salt and water only, e.g. metal oxides.

Carnivore Animal that eats other animals.

Cell (electrical) Source of power. The cell produces an electric current from the reaction taking place inside it.

Cell membrane Thin skin that surrounds the cytoplasm of the cell.

Cells Tiny units that make up living matter.

Cervix Part of the female reproductive system.

Chemical reaction Change that results in the formation of new substances. Usually cannot be reversed.

Chromatography Method of separating mixtures dissolved in a solvent.

Circuit diagram Shows position of electrical objects, e.g. lamp, resistor in a circuit through which current can flow.

Compound Two or more substances joined together that cannot easily be separated.

Constriction (narrowing) connecting the vagina to the uterus.

Consumer Organism that eats other living things (animals or plants).

Crustacean Arthropod having two pairs of antennae, nine to 15 pairs of legs and often a hard, chalky shell.

Current A flow of electrical charge.

Cytoplasm Jelly-like substance that fills most of a cell.

Density The mass of one unit of volume of a substance.

Diffusion Movement of particles from where they are highly concentrated to where they are less concentrated.

Distillation Method of separating two liquids that have different boiling points.

Electrical circuit Source of power such as a battery connected to other components arranged so that a current can flow.

Embryo Name for the developing baby during the first eight weeks of pregnancy.

Energy Quantity that enables objects to do something or make something.

Evaporation Physical change that, by using heat, turns a liquid into a gas.

External fertilisation Egg(s) is fertilised outside the female.

Fertilisation Joining together of a male sex cell with a female sex cell.

Fetus (foetus) Name for developing baby from eight weeks of pregnancy up to birth.

Food chain Series of organisms that eat and are eaten by each other. Green plants always start a food chain.

Force Something that can pull, push, twist, turn and change the speed and direction of movement.

Fossil fuels Fuels, e.g. coal and gas, made millions of years ago from dead plants and animals. They all contain carbon.

Friction Force between two objects when they slide over each other.

Fuel Substance that burns easily to produce heat and light.

Fuse Acts to break an electrical circuit.

Gas One of the three states of matter. In a gas the distances between particles are large.

Gravity Attractive force of a body for a nearby object. The more massive the body the stronger the gravitational force.

Habitat Place where organisms live. It supplies food, shelter and an area to breed.

Herbivore Animal that eats only plants, e.g. cow.

Hibernation Way of avoiding harsh conditions by sleeping for long periods.

Indicator Liquid that can change colour and therefore indicate if something is acid or alkaline.

Inherit Acquire characteristics from parents.

Insoluble Substance that will not dissolve in a particular solvent.

Insulation Acts to keep the temperature of a body constant.

Internal fertilisation Egg(s) is fertilised inside the female.

Invertebrates Animals without a backbone.

Kingdoms Way of classifying living things. There are five kingdoms: animals, plants, fungi, moneta (bacteria) and protoctists (simple single-celled organisms).

Liquid One of the three states of matter. The particles are only loosely attached to one another so that liquids can flow easily.

Luminous Giving out light.

Mammals Class of animals that suckle their young.

Mass Amount of matter in a material.

Menstrual cycle Occurs in fertile human females. Normally about 28 days in length, an ovum ripens and is released during each cycle.

Menstruation Another word for period. It is the time in the **menstrual cycle** when the uterus lining breaks down and passes out through the vagina.

Metal Element that is hard, shiny and conducts heat and electricity.

Metamorphosis When a living organism changes its form completely, e.g. tadpole and frog.

Migration Way of avoiding harsh conditions by moving to a new habitat.

Nervous tissue Made of nerve cells. Carries impulses (messages) around the body.

Neutralisation Reaction where an acid is cancelled out by a base.

Newton Unit of force.

Non-luminous Object that does not give out light.

Non-renewable fuel Fuel that cannot be replaced, e.g. coal, oil and gas.

Nucleus Controls the activities of the cell.

Omnivore Animal that eats animals and plants.

Organ Group of tissues.

Ovaries Female sex organs that produce ova.

Oviducts Part of the female reproductive system. Two long tubes connecting the ovaries to the uterus.

Ovum Female sex cell, sometimes called an egg.

Parallel circuit Each electrical object in the circuit can be switched on or off without affecting the other objects in the circuit.

Period Another word for **menstruation**.

pH Measure of the acidity or alkalinity of a liquid.

pH scale Scale of 1 to 14, with pH 7 (neutral) at its centre.

Photosynthesis Process by which plants use the energy from the Sun to change carbon dioxide and water into oxygen and food.

Physical change Process in which no new substance is made. The change can easily be reversed.

Placenta The organ of exchange of substances, e.g. oxygen and nutrients, between the mother and the growing fetus.

Predator Preys on other living things.

Producer Organism at start of a food chain. Plants are producers.

Products Chemicals on the right-hand side of a chemical equation.

Puberty The onset of adolescence when the sex organs become fully developed.

Reactants Chemicals on the left-hand side of a chemical equation.

Reactivity A measure of how likely a substance is to react (change).

Renewable fuel Fuel that can be replaced, e.g. wood, wind and solar.

Resistance (ohms) Opposition to a current in a circuit by a material.

Rusting Process in which air and water react with iron.

Series circuit Electrical circuit with all the components connected one after another.

Solid One of the three states of matter. The particles vibrate in fixed positions.

Soluble Describes a substance that dissolves.

Solute Substance that dissolves in a solvent to form a solution.

Solution Formed when a solute dissolves in a solvent.

Solvent Liquid in which the solute dissolves.

Suspension Formed when an insoluble substance is added to water, e.g. muddy water.

Testes Part of the male reproductive system. Make sperm.

Tissues Group of similar cells, which perform similar tasks.

Umbilical cord Part of the developing fetus. Connects fetus to mother's placenta.

Uterus Part of the female reproductive system. Provides a place for growing fetus.

Vacuole Fluid-filled space inside a cell.

Variation Difference in offspring of the same parents.

Vertebrates Animals with a backbone. There are five groups: fish, amphibians, reptiles, birds and mammals.

Voltage (volts) The pushing force in an electrical circuit.

Volume The space occupied by a contained substance.

Weight Force caused by gravity.

Answers to puzzles

Wanted – do you recognise this cell?   **p. 5**

'Little units of life'   **p. 7**

Feature	Does it occur in plant cells?	Does it occur in animal cells?
cell wall	✓	✗
cell membrane	✓	✓
cytoplasm	✓	✓
chloroplast	✓	✗
nucleus	✓	✓
vacuole	✓	✗

HEART; LUNGS; BLADDER; MUSCLES; OVARIES
ALL LIVING THINGS ARE MADE OF CELLS

All change!   **p. 9**
A James; B George; C Daniel; D Alison; E Mary

a) (i) 9 years; (ii) 10, 11, 12 (iii) Puberty in girls starts before boys; b) 13 cm

Baby talk   **p. 11**
2 3 5 1 4; 2 4 1 3

Animal magic   **p. 15**
1 kingfisher; 2 frog; 3 spawn; 4 hamster; 5 guppies

1 dog, hamster, guppy, human; 2 guppy, frog; 3 human; 4 frog

Home, sweet home   **p. 17**
A E F G L O R S
FROG SEAL

1 habitat
2 a) migrate; b) water; c) hibernating; d) fins; e) hair

Who ate Peter Pigeon?   **p. 19**
grass → worm → pigeon → fox

CATERPILLAR; SPARROW; HAWK; TREE

TREE → CATERPILLAR → SPARROW → HAWK
Producer is TREE

Variety is the spice of life   **p. 23**

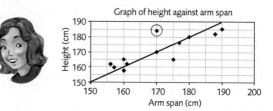

a) 165 cm; b) (i) 4; (ii) 5; c) see graph; d) equal

In a class of their own   **p. 25**
KINGDOMS

carnivore: dragonfly nymph, watermite
herbivore: mayfly nymph
plant: duckweed, pondweed
omnivore: goldfish, water boatman

Bitter sweet   **p. 29**
ACETIC ASCORBIC CITRIC
AMMONIA DETERGENT

A	A	C
C	B	B
B	A	A
B	B	C

Indicators   **p. 31**
RED ORANGE YELLOW GREEN
BLUE INDIGO VIOLET

1 (i) pH less than 7, e.g. tea; (ii) pH greater than 7, e.g. detergent; (iii) pH = 7, e.g. water
2 oven cleaner/soap flakes
3 lemon juice
4 (i) red; (ii) blue

A neutral solution   **p. 33**
Fire hazard below 23 °C. Extremely hazardous. Shock or heat may explode it. Do not use water.

Add damp litmus paper, turns blue if calcium oxide present; no change of colour with talcum powder.

What's done cannot be undone   **p. 37**
Reading vertically downwards paw prints are: rabbit; (fox); dog; squirrel; badger; cat

a) C; b) C; c) C; d) P; e) P

Show your metal — p. 39

1 zinc; 2 gold; 3 iron; 4 copper; 5 potassium; 6 sodium; 7 magnesium; 8 lead; 9 aluminium; 10 platinum

a) iron; b) aluminium; c) copper; d) silver/gold/platinum; e) (i) hydrogen; (ii) oxygen

Burning the candle at both ends — p. 41

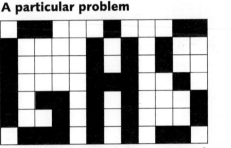

1 oxygen; 2 $750\ cm^3$; 3 11 s

A particular problem — p. 45

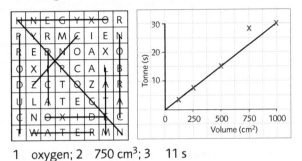

1 solid; 2 gas; 3 gas can be compressed; pressure is transmitted through a liquid; 4 tiny particles of cut grass diffuse through the air particles

A possible solution — p. 47

SOLUTE

1 (i) salt; (ii) water
2 I I I S; S S I I
3 (i) crush it; (ii) heat it; (iii) stir it

Cheque it out — p. 49

1 (ROOT); 2 CAT; 3 GOAT; 4 TORCH; 5 MORTAR; 6 CARROT; 7 MOTOR CAR

a) 4; b) red, blue, green; c) orange; d) position on chromatogram

A burning issue — p. 51

NON-RENEWABLE; 2 WATER; 3 GEOLOGY
ENERGY

1 FUEL; 2 HEAT; 3 SOLAR; 4 RENEWABLE; 5 WAVES

Circuit training — p. 55

(CELL); CIRCUIT; ELECTRICITY; LAMP; PARALLEL; POSITIVE; SERIES; SWITCH; TERMINAL; WIRE

1 (i) radio; (ii) TV; (iii) microwave, etc.

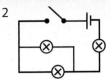

Lighting up — p. 57

P		L				F	
A	O	A			C	U	
R	H	M		S	U	S	
A	M	P	E	R	E		
L				R	R		
L				I	E		
E				E	N		
L				S	T		

1 (i) amps; (ii) volts; (iii) ohms
2 fuse blows, or mcb is tripped
3 decrease

Can you resist it? — p. 59

BATTERIES 1 none; 2 A B; 3 A; 4 A C

Don't force it! — p. 63

PUSH; PULL; SIZE; FORCE; ARROW; WEIGHT
larger arrows: bird, ball, rocket, gravity, arm of winner; *can't tell:* rugby game

A dense topic — p. 65

(1 GRAVITY); 2 MASS; 3 MOON; 4 EARTH; 5 NEWTON; 6 WEIGHT; 7 DENSITY; 8 FORCE; 9 KILOGRAM; 10 VOLUME

1 apple; cork; plastic ball; 2 helium gas is less dense than air; carbon dioxide is denser than air; 3 $4\ g/cm^3$

Friction forces — p. 67

FRICTION 1 top line; 2 friction is reduced when wet; friction increases with weight.

Worlds apart — p. 71

ASTEROID; PLANET; COMET; SATELLITE; MOON; STAR
1 The Sun casts a shadow of the Earth on the Moon
2 28 days; 3 reflects light from Sun
4 a) equal one another; b) missions to the Moon

The final frontier — p. 73

N	E	P	T	U	N	E				

(crossword of planets)
U R A N U S
S A T U R N
J U P I T E R
V E N U S
M E R C U R Y
E A R T H
M A R S
N E P T U N E

1 a) planets; 2 Pluto; 3 gravity of the Sun; 4 Mercury

Test your knowledge 1

1 a)

b) (i) (ii) chloroplast, cell wall, vacuole

2 ovary, uterus, period, 28, puberty, pregnant, baby

3 F M; Shape of body, females have narrower waists and wider hips than men.
boys: any two from height increases; penis grows; pubic hair grows; hair on face and chest; more muscular; shoulders broader; voice breaks
girls: any two from height increases; breasts grow; pubic hair grows; hips widen and get rounder; periods begin

4 D C B A

Test your knowledge 2

1 a) (i) mice; (ii) earthworm/slugs; (iii) grass/dead leaves, fox (iv) dead leaves, spiders, pigeons;
b) oak tree; c) (i) pigeons, hedgehogs; (ii) fox; d) mouse

2 a) amphibian; b) webbed feet, streamlined body; c) get away from predators, swim quickly after prey; d) (i) externally; (ii) so some survive; (iii) hard to swallow/slippery/horrible taste; e) row 1: decreases; row 2 decreases; row 3: increases, increases

Test your knowledge 3

1 a) nose, brown eyes, black; b) scar, height, language, hair length; c) (i) 36; d) weight, arm span

2 B A C D E F
A earthworm; B snail; D spider; E woodlouse

Test your knowledge 4

1 a) (i) alkaline; (ii) pH of 9, not poisonous;
b) (i) pH just greater than 7, not poisonous
c) a suspension separates into solid and liquid if left to stand, a mixture stays mixed

2 a) blue; purple; yellow; colourless; b) (green) red (orange) colourless acidic; blue (blue) yellow red alkaline; (yellow) red red colourless (acidic); blue (purple) yellow colourless neutral; blue blue yellow (red) alkaline; c) 7; d) red; e) use a pH meter

Test your knowledge 5

1 a) hydrogen; b) makes salt dissolve more quickly; c) (i) carbon/graphite (ii) salt solution; (iii) salt; d) (i) reacted with water to give hydrogen and alkaline solution; (ii) burns to give oxide with pH less than 7; (iii) burned to form two compounds (elements would give one)

2 a) (i) milk, butter, eggs; (ii) flour, sugar; (iii) salt; (iv) baking powder; b) (i) 12; (ii) baking powder, sugar; c) heat it; d) cannot be reversed, new substance formed; e) ✓ ✓ ✗ ✗

Test your knowledge 6

1 a)

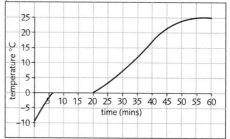

b) (i) –10 °C; (ii) 25 °C; c) (i) C; (ii) B; d) (i) less dense than water; (ii) the molecules are further apart in ice than in water

2 a) 90%; b) (i) heat; (ii) light; c) cannot be replaced; d) solar

Test your knowledge 7

1 another bulb, steel papers clip, pencil lead, silver spoon, another cell

2 a) (i) 1; (ii) 1 and 2; (iii) 3; (iv) 2; b) red and green

3 a) Type 1: series circuit, Type 2: parallel circuit (see diagrams on p54); b) if bulb blows, rest of lights stay on; c) more resistance in circuit

Test your knowledge 8

1 a) push, direction, weight, Earth, gravity, size, stationary, move; b) the ball starts dropping (force of gravity); c) (i) both arrows equal; (ii) down arrow larger than up; (iii) forward arrow greater than backward

2 a) (i) kg; (ii) Newtons; b) Moon has less mass; c) (i) friction; (ii) friction reduced

3 down, forwards, backwards and down

Test your knowledge 9

1 a)

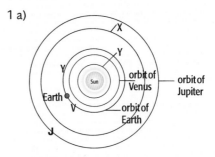

b) reflect light from the Sun; c) sometimes near sometimes far away from Earth; d) (ii) nearer to Earth; e) far side of Earth not receiving any light

2 a) (i) 31; (ii) 8; b) (i) 365; (ii) lunar month is 28 days 365 ÷ 28 ≈ 13; c) 21 June

(i)

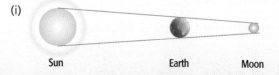

Sun   Earth   Moon

d) Sun Earth Moon; (ii) same diagram; (iii) Earth larger than Moon; e) there is a new Moon